# PLEASE LEAD US IN PRAYER

# PLEASE LEAD US IN PRAYER

Norman L. Cullumber

The Bethany Press
St. Louis, Missouri

Scripture quotations, unless otherwise noted, are from the Revised Standard Version of the Bible, copyrighted 1946, 1952, © 1971, 1973 by the Division of Christian Education of the National Council of the Churches of Christ in the U.S.A., and are used by permission.

Library of Congress Cataloging in Publication Data

Cullumber, Norman L.
    Please Lead Us in Prayer
    1. Prayer.      2. Prayers.    I. Title.
    BV 226. C84    264'. 1         80-105 31


ISBN 0-8272-2928-3

Distributed in Canada by The G. R. Welch Company, Ltd., Toronto, Ontario, Canada


Printed in the United States of America

# Contents

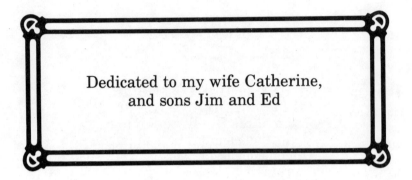

Dedicated to my wife Catherine,
and sons Jim and Ed

# Foreword

"Please lead us in prayer!"

When this request zips across the room to Hal Smith, he breaks out in a cold sweat. Joe Coreyander gets trembly knees when he gets the call, and Jill Mills crosses her fingers behind her back when her turn comes. These are the many lay persons who know they should always be ready to lead in public prayer, but who would like a little help.

"I don't know what words to use," confesses one church person from a denomination that has no prayer book to guide her. Another asks, "What shall I pray for?" "I don't know where to begin," chimes in a new deacon. "Our lay people are sincere and dedicated," says an intelligent young woman from First Church, "but the prayers of our elders at the communion table ramble and are too long. Isn't there some way our leaders can lead us without preaching a sermon in the prayers?"

With little formal theological training and limited public speaking experience, leaders may be tempted to "cover the waterfront" in their public prayers. While they are talking to God, they are also teaching their congregation concepts of God and how we come to him. Therefore, when they lead in public prayer they are sharing their faith.

This book is designed to help lay persons develop skill in leading public prayer. The different parts and moods of prayer are brought into sharp focus, and the steps of forming public prayers are outlined. Different occasions and diverse groups are highlighted along with unique settings and customary events. The use of imagination and creativity are important ingredients to the story of good public prayer.

The model prayers are arranged and composed so they can be taken directly from the book for use at the appropriate time. Or they may be modified to suit special needs.

Prayers from books should be eventual doorways through which the individual's own prayers can stride purposefully. Above all, we echo the disciples' plea to Jesus: "Lord, teach us to pray."

# CHAPTER 1

FOUNDATIONS OF PUBLIC PRAYER: GOD
AND HIS PEOPLE
    God and his family, the church
    Definitions and purpose of public prayer
    Dimensions of prayer: for what should I
    pray?

YOUR CHANCE to lead in public prayer may come at any time and with fascinating results.

A layman in a small town called in a home where there had been a death. The teenage son of a widow had been killed in a tragic auto accident the night before, and although no one in the family was a member of his congregation, the churchman wanted to express his sympathy.

After a few awkward attempts at conversation with the tearful family, he suggested a prayer. With no pretense at oratory, he prayed like this:

> Our Father, we thank you that you are always near and that you love us. Will you make this family aware that you are close now and that you are their Friend who suffers with them? In Jesus' name, Amen.

Then he silently clasped the grieving mother's hand and left. Weeks later he was met on the street by a member of the family who wanted to thank him for his visit.

"You didn't have to come," she said, "but we were glad you did. And I especially want to thank you for your prayer. It reminded us of some things we had forgotten and needed to remember."

The layman could have responded that prayer plays that part in the Christian's life. Prayer is an inseparable part of the human family's life when the meaning of prayer is understood. When people are sad or when they are happy, there is the need for prayer. When the situation is rough they kneel for a word with God. When rescue comes, that same urge to give thanks calls for a prayer. If persons are hurt beyond human repair, what is more natural than to turn to someone nearby and ask for a prayer? Prayer is the healing and therapy the mind and emotions need.

What better place is there to see this than in a typical congregation? On a Sunday morning any church has a variety of persons coming with secret anxieties to find solutions to tough, unyielding problems. And in most churches there are persons carrying hidden sins and shame that make life a constant sentence of guilt. The gathered Christians' needs serve as a stimulus for the making of sensitive prayers and are a reminder that prayer for many is a life and death issue.

Here is a man who hopes that his drinking escapades are not a prelude to crippling alcoholism. In moments when he is sober, he is often worried about his increasing dependence on liquor, but if he were confronted he would angrily deny any such problem exists, that he "can take it or leave it alone." He needs the therapy of prayer.

Or there is a woman who is thinking of abandoning her family and the monotony of thankless household chores. She dreams of a free and fancy life where all is glamour and excitement. She has an offer that would make this all apparently come true and she has to decide quickly what course her future will take. Prayer helps clear her mind as she chooses.

An embittered daughter comes to church bringing her anger with her. Her aged mother will soon have to be placed in a nursing home because the daughter can no longer provide the needed care. However, her sisters and brothers accuse her of a callous disregard for her mother's feelings and criticize her in the presence of other members of the family. The bitterness is sharper because she feels she has to provide her mother's care all alone. Prayer puts her in touch with the God who knows all about forgiving those who wrongfully use others.

A youth sits in his pew furiously fuming because he was denied the use of the family car the night before to go out with some friends, but is forced to go to church. He needs prayer's calm perspective.

Anger, bitterness, resentment, unfulfilled dreams and anxiety, as well as hope, happiness, love and trust are all the feelings of the family of God, the church. So these emotional needs must be dealt with in prayer in the ordinary language of those who share these feelings in their everyday experiences. The clamor and clutter of work and play are shut out for a moment as we become aware we are in the presence of Someone who makes sense of it all and understands the intensity of all these experiences and moods.

It is human living and its ups and downs that are the ingredients of which prayer is made. This relationship between prayer and life is reflected in the times prayer finds its way into the morning worship of a congregation, for Christian life is indeed anemic if prayer is removed. The basic kinship between God and the family of God is stated and restated and made fresh and new through public prayer. The words of the leader are the channel through which the family conversation is flowing, and if prayer is led properly, God's power is brought to bear on human life to make it strong and courageous.

The practical expression of the importance of prayer is seen in the way in which the church builds prayer into its worship. A look at a Sunday worship bulletin demonstrates how a congregation feels about the need for a variety of prayers. The invocation is at the beginning; it asks God to make his presence known; about midway in the service the pastoral prayer lifts the needs and hopes of the people. Most services close with either a prayer or benediction. A scan of the order of worship may reveal other prayers at the high points of the worship hour.

Early in its history the church understood that Jesus' life was radiant because of his praying, and the church found that the life Christ gave to others was strong and vigorous because it was nourished by regular and consistent prayer. The unmistakable impact prayer made was soon noticed by those around Jesus; it could not remain hidden because Jesus obviously possessed something so unique in the quality of his living that the whole countryside marveled. Jesus prayed with a stunning sense of assurance that God heard and would answer. That sense of confidence has been needed in every age.

However, our experience teaches us that the answer we get may not coincide with our expressed desires. If we do not lose patience with prayer, we learn eventually that the answer we get is the response we need.

God's answering our prayers is a good deal like the story heard recently of the father who was asked by each of his two sons for a sizable loan.

The younger son, who had been a cripple during childhood, wanted the money to move to a city where he had a new job. The other son had been an athlete and popular in school and had "breezed" through college. He wanted to go on a tour with his loan.

The father carefully assessed the needs of each and made his decision. To the younger son who had been a cripple, he gave the money instead of loaning it. To the popular, athletic brother he gave—directions to the bank where he could borrow the money on his own!

In the wholesome family relationship the wise parent knows the best for each child and gives what is needed regardless of what the youngster wants. That is because the wisdom of the

11

parent insists that necessities are more critical to the well being of the young person than childish desires. That is the way God deals with his family. His concern is that each gets that which is good and necessary for growth and development, that which provides the long run care. Because God's love goes beyond the whimsies of the moment, he helps persons have the experiences that call for maturity and responsibility.

Because these experiences vary among individuals, those who gather for public worship will come in all sorts of mental and spiritual conditions. They need public prayer that enables each of them to find a place within the prayer to God. If they can find prayer which speaks for them in all their diversity they become participants rather than spectators. Instead of being an audience, they have a role in the drama. In all their differences they are united because it is their prayer and not just their leader's.

Here is a prayer that we used at the close of a meeting which brought a hundred or so persons from widespread sections of a large city. They were delegates who had been called to conduct the business of the church. The leader sought to avoid sexist terms in the prayer.

Our Heavenly Parent, we thank you for all these who have come to bring their talents and who have invested their time for the business of your kingdom. We come from many parts of our area because of our deep concern and keen interest in your work. We hope that our words and deeds will bring light and hope to those who suffer.

We ask you to bless us each by giving us the wisdom and insight we need to live faithfully as your people in all the changes and challenges of this age.

As we go our separate ways, we ask you to keep each one safe, but if we cannot be safe, then save us by the power of your presence, through Jesus Christ, Amen.

This prayer, in addition to greeting God, has three distinct parts. In the first, the oneness or family-like quality of the group is stressed and there is an affirmation of the mission

12

mind of the meeting. The leader moves on then to ask for a blessing which is tangible and which carefully avoids asking for God's favor in general. The leader frames what is being sought in specific terms. Finally, there is a benediction for the safekeeping of the members and a statement of faith in the sufficiency of God's power to save his people. The prayer is direct and to the point. Members of the group are asked to join hands to symbolize their unity.

Your own spiritual preparation for the task of leading in prayer should not be neglected as the beginning point of forming public prayer that lets God and his people find their meeting place in your words. The fact that you are called to lead in public prayer does not lessen your own humanity. For you to lead in prayer is to declare your own participation in the life of the family of God as an individual. It says that you share in the struggle and joy of being alive as do those whom you lead. The leader cannot be detached from those whose thoughts are being directed. Instead, the guide is in the center of whatever struggle or celebration is occurring. For a moment you are singled out to describe, to declare, to ask, to share the abundance of God's love. Your selection as leader is always tempered by your awareness that the leader is not greater than those being led. Humility is a key to good prayer leadership.

As you are planning to share in some group worship, it would be good for you to start your day by thinking of some of the things you have learned about God. It may be his love, or some special way he shows his power or wisdom. You could reflect on the fact that he holds together a universe that provides for all life's needs. Consider how his completeness is mirrored in his creation. You may want to begin the day with an inventory of those friends through whom you have come to know God and in whose deeds you see Godlike acts occurring.

Then use your imagination to concentrate on the fact that he wants to use you and your talents to bring healing and hope to those present at the event. History is filled with the stories of those chosen by God to be his leaders.

You might want to think of some of the great heroes of the Bible or the church. As you ponder how God has used them, ask if he can use you in your time and place in a way of his choosing. Offer yourself for that mission. Remember, God has the power to take that which seems small and insignificant and transform it into something uniquely useful. Quietly imagine that he takes your hand and sets you before your group. You know he is there with you. You move and speak in the steady confidence of one who is aware that God is close by.

The ability to lead in prayer is strengthened by familiarity with the Bible and its stirring drama of life. Sensitivity to the needs of people and great prayers that provide hope and sanity are found on page after page. While we do not want to adopt the language of the Old and New Testaments, it is helpful to become acquainted with biblical persons as men and women of prayer.

For example, the great prayer of Jesus for his church, which you can read in the seventeenth chapter of John, demonstrates the care Christian minds have for one another and sets the example for Christian concern.

The simple prayer of the prophet Elisha—when surrounded by a mighty army seeking his life—can introduce you to prayer in time of distress and turmoil. These astounding events are found in 2 Kings 6:11 ff.

Or what is the discussion between Moses and God on Sinai except prayer? Look at the story in Exodus 19 and you will see how Moses' prayer is a conversation with God. Did you ever stop to think that it is through the medium of prayer that God delivers his Law? Thus the many sides of prayer become apparent when we read through the scriptures and see how prayer relates persons to God and how God finds his people.

As you read and study scripture, it will become increasingly evident to you that your growing acquaintance with the experience of the biblical story not only will enliven your ability to be in front of persons, but also will help you make their needs a part of the prayer you lead.

This intimate contact with the great pray-ers of the Bible also reveals the things which are good topics for public prayer. If your denomination has a prescribed liturgy or prayer book, your prayer is already composed. Topics are included in the designated prayer after careful thought by your church and you can rely on these prayers to include subjects that reflect a mature and seasoned understanding of Christian prayer. Prayers that have survived the test of time are likely to be included in your prayer book and these can help you have insight into the petitions and thoughts that ought to go into public prayer.

If you are using a prayer from the prayer book, give the prayer a careful initial reading out loud to catch the flow of ideas and to highlight the structure. Look at the phrases, the movement from subject to subject, and the use of words. Observe how the descriptive adjectives and the action verbs go together to make color and vitality.

Prayer books and service books are found in the Episcopal Church, the Presbyterian Church, the Lutheran Church, and the United Methodist Church as well as others who use them on occasion. Since the framers of these prayers have outlined exceptional petitions that are classics for simplicity and beauty, it would help to have these on hand to use in your study of public prayer.

Such prayers should serve as a stimulus to your own thinking if you come from a church that does not rely on books of prayers. By being aware of the selfless quality of these prayers, you can compose your own prayer that embodies the same concepts. Moreover, you become alerted to how prayers are fitted into services with different themes. You will catch something of the timelessness of the church and you will see how God is active in the different expressions of the church.

You will come to see that the classical prayers ask for what we need and for what we should be. You will discover how prayer is a search for a better world, a more Christ-like life and a vision for a world to come. Shouldn't these elements always be present in whatever prayers we offer?

When you are asked to lead in public prayer, you may be told that the prayer you are to lead is to be printed, either in the book of worship or in the church's worship bulletin. If that is the case, a part of your responsibility is to preview the prayer to make it yours. Become familiar with the words of the prayer as soon as possible so your reading will not be forced or false. Practice with the prayer until you have clearly in mind what words are to be emphasized. You can experiment to see how shifting the emphasis alters the meaning and mood. By all means avoid the monotone, but also beware of becoming too dramatic or adopting a "prayer tone" to your voice. A tape recorder can be helpful at this point. Work with the prayer until it sounds natural to your ears. This advance work keeps the mechanics of the prayer's delivery from being prominent and from calling attention to yourself. It helps focus the congregation on God.

But let us suppose your denomination does not have prescribed prayers, or you are asked at an informal meeting to lead in prayer and you have no prayer to read. What then? For what should you pray, and what safeguards are there to help you form thoughtful prayers?

We need to look closely at that question because we are uncomfortable when a well-meaning person asks God for something we suspect will not be in the best interests of the recipient. In some instances persons are embarrassed by a prayer that directs God to do what the pray-er wants without regard to the divine will, or by a prayer which irreverently implies that God really doesn't know the whole story of what is happening.

It is when we begin to form prayers that we are all theologians. That is, we have a set of beliefs about God and the way he works. Sometimes we are quite conscious of these principles and we can make a system of them and have them in order. During our work and everyday life, our family and social experiences, we more or less follow the consequences of these beliefs about God. We behave and speak in such a way as to follow what belief urges. When we step out of bounds, we are painfully aware that word or deed is inconsistent with our faith. In leading in public prayer these principles are an unconscious but important part of our thinking. We reflect our faith in our prayers.

Imagine that you are visiting a very sick friend in the hospital. You understand that the illness is quite serious and there is a good chance that your friend will not recover. Surgery is indicated and if successful, a long period of recuperation is to follow. A relative at the bedside asks you for a word of prayer. What will you say?

It is here that your thinking about God and how he deals with people becomes extremely important. Here is a prayer for use on such an occasion. As you read the prayer, see if you can determine the thoughts behind the phrases that reflect what the pray-er believed about God.

Our Father who is always present, we are grateful that you reach into hospitals where there is pain and suffering. We are thankful that you are here, too, because our need for you is multiplied by John's sickness.

We appreciate this hospital, its staff of doctors and nurses, those who care for us, and who have given years of study to prepare to provide us that care. Thank you for using them to bring healing.

16

All healing and health ultimately come from you, O God, and we are convinced of your care for us because of your Son, Jesus Christ, who demonstrates your concern.

As our friend faces the days ahead, will you make his life full with your support? Will you minister to him through those who you have called? We do not know what these days will bring, but our faith is in you. We reach out to take your hand in the trust that all is well in your care. In Jesus' name, Amen.

The person who led this prayer in the sickroom was conscious of the phrase in the Lord's Prayer, ".....thy kingdom come, thy will be done..." Although his friend's well-being was prominent is his mind, the leader assumed God was capable and sufficient. So the leader did not dwell on the details of the friend's ailment. Rather, he dealt with the issues of faith that all persons face in moments such as those. He was making a prayer of proclamation. He affirmed that God made his way into the whole healing process of which the patient's faith and the hospital staff's skills are such important parts. He was saying that God heals through trained and dedicated people. And he was following his belief that God was the God who wanted his people well and healed.

Some who have rejected prayer have done so because well-meaning persons have advised them to pray for whatever they wanted. No matter how extreme their desires, they would get their wishes if they only prayed with enough faith! Having their wants denied, they have then been accused of lacking a proper amount of trust!

This is an abuse of prayer. Prayer is not magic, nor is it a means of manipulating God into doing what we want. Prayer is answered in many fashions. "No," may be one response, or the reply coud be, "You have prayed for too little. I want you to have more and better than you asked, but in a different way than you thought." Or, "Wait awhile," might be heard. Prayer calls for readiness to receive the answer best suited to meet human need.

When these specific needs are mentioned in public prayer, the leader wants to keep clearly in mind that he or she states these as a part of the family conversation with the Father who is already quite aware of them. The circle of Christian love makes these needs the needs of the group. The character of loving concern makes many topics fit subjects for prayer that might otherwise appear unworthy of being included.

Prayer, then, ought always help life fit into the kind of conduct and faith that we are intended to have and which is so amply illustrated by the life of Jesus Christ. You need to be conscious that your words are lifting your members from preoccupation with their problems to the resources that God offers. Public prayer is a light focused for a moment on the help that is so near, yet so unseen.

# ADDITIONAL PRAYERS

## Where there has been a death

O GOD, who knowest our deepest thoughts and feelings, we come in this hour of sadness to seek the consoling guidance and help that cometh only from thee as we bear the loss of our loved one. In this moment when the darkness of grief closes about us we think of our Friend who said, "I am the resurrection and the life; he who believes in me, though he die, yet shall he live, and whoever lives and believes in me shall never die."

We are thankful for him who stands beside us in our sorrow and for thee who hath known the death of thy Son and so knowest our pain. But even as thou dost share our affliction, so also dost thou share the joy of resurrection by thy Son, Jesus Christ. As by him we know the reality of death, so also by him do we come to understand the victory of life that comes by thy power.

For now, Father, surround us with the loving arms of thy care, that in our desolation we might not be alone nor feel forsaken. And in the time to come, sustain and strengthen our faith so that one day all the darkness of death will be swept away. Help us to etch the precious memories of life with (him/her) deeply into our minds until that day when we again meet face to face, through Jesus Christ, our Lord, Amen.

ETERNAL FATHER, strong to save, the awesome mystery of death has swept suddenly through this family circle, and we are left devastated by its passing. It has robbed us of one whom we loved dearly and in (his/her) place has left the chilling numbness of shock and grief. We do not understand, and our thoughts pile up one upon another, until we are confused and weak. There was so much we wanted to do and say, but now all our desires seem so futile and empty, so wasted.

But in our moments when it seems the darkest, we look, and lo, you come to us, walking toward us over the storm and peril of our loss, and we hear your voice, "Take heart; it is I; have no fear." And just as ancient seas subsided and tumults ceased at the word of your Christ, so does our storm of doubt and fear grow calm and there is peace. _____(name)_____ has contributed so much to the good of the world; so let us build on (his/her) deeds and by our work for a better world so let us express our love and affection. Help us to forge a life based on noble principles and steadfast righteousness. Enable us to seek good for our neighbor and to teach others by our example so that your Kingdom will grow in the minds of all that we encounter.

Touch us, O God, and remind us you are near in Christ; Amen.

OUR FATHER, we need you so much in this hour! The harsh intruder, Death, has invaded us and taken one from our midst. All that we sought to do was to no avail and we were helpless as little children confronted by some monstrous evil. The word you have given us through your Son, Jesus Christ, reminds us of your presence and your caring and your desire to lift our burdens, so we turn to you in the hope that we shall not feel so alone.

Touch our spirits, O Father, that even in this dark time we shall appreciate the gift of _____(name)_____ whom you have given to us to love and cherish. As time passes and blunts the edge of our grief, we shall not forget the dreams and aspirations that (he/she) held dearly. Nor shall we fail to remember the high moments of joy and the rich times of happiness as we shared ourselves with each other in the selflessness that love brings. As we struggle to make sense of these happenings, quicken our faith. Keep us from hasty conclusions or self-imposed feelings of guilt, and help us through our own valley of the shadow of death as we seek to live.

It is you, O God, who alone can bring order out of chaos, peace out of turmoil, sunshine out of darkness. We trust you. Amen.

## In the hospital or home where there is illness

O GOOD and great Physician, we place ourselves in your hands as we struggle for health in the midst of illness. Truly you are the one in whom all health lies and from you comes every good and perfect gift.

O Father, may those who feel pain know the ease of healing, and may those persons who suffer know the return of strength and vitality. Help those who are anxious about surgery (or treatment) face tomorrow with the calm assurance of those who know in whose hands they are as your children.

You work in so many ways to bring health, O God, that we marvel at all you do for your people. Science kneels at your feet to be obedient to your wish that all have good health, or learn to live victoriously with health that is poor.

Enable the sick, then, to be a part of the great healing process by being well in mind and spirit, though ill of body. Grant patience if healing is slow and give strength against doubt and despair. Encourage them by the discovery that you are by their side and make them an encouragement to others, too, for yours is the kingdom and the power and the glory for ever, Amen.

HEAVENLY FATHER, grant that healing may come and pain may abate. If it is your will, restore to health _____(name)_____ and set (him/her) in the midst of (his/her) family again, through Jesus our Lord, Amen.

## In times of crisis: making big decisions

**O** God, whose very presence is light, shine into our lives this day, for great decisions have to be made. Commitments are to be given and promises extended; we have come to a crossroad where we must choose and select a way from the several ways that confront us, and we are not sure which is the best. Others depend on us and their future will be shaped by options we pick. We are aware of the responsibility that is ours.

Will you touch our minds with wisdom and give us the capacity to have insight into implications of our choices? Will you help us have clarity of thought and sharpness of reason that our choices will reflect your will? May we have the mind of Christ, so that whatever we choose we might be in keeping with those things that he taught. For we ask this in his name, Amen.

## In times of crisis: when a family is on the brink of dividing

OUR GOD and Parent, whose love made our lives possible, and who has called all persons to be your family, some face division and brokenness of relationship where the love that once bound persons together has been fractured and legal separation seems eminent. Once where joy ruled there is now sadness and personal hurt.

O God, whose Son forgave even those who sought his life, teach us that same kind of love that penetrates through the hot and hasty words to blunt the edge of bitterness and restore the affection that brings persons close. May our hurt feelings and selfishness plunge into the depths of Christ's love, to emerge as kindness to each other and sacrificial giving, one to the other. By the power of your Holy Spirit put the pieces of our lives back into one portrait of harmony and caring, through Jesus Christ, Amen.

## In times of crisis: when someone is striving for mental health

O GOD, whose Christ took persons whose minds were shattered and brought wholeness, we pray for those who seek to be whole of mind and spirit. We know some who strive to gain control of impulses and urges that seem to run wild, while others are ruled by habits instead of reason and good judgment. You enable us to see ourselves as we really are in your eyes, persons of great worth and value. You are reflected in us, and you have made us each uniquely your own. So for those whose minds are stormy or depressed, bring a true sense of proportion and meaning. Help them find the balance to walk through the time of threat that will make them victors. Make your people competent to live in a world of threat without fear, and to face the demands of this time with courage. In the spirit of Christ, Amen.

# CHAPTER 2

DEVELOPING A STYLE OF PUBLIC PRAYER
    Matching your prayer to the occasion
    Choosing and using a theme
    To write or not to write?
    The language of public prayer

AT SOME point in your participation in the life of the church the request that you lead in public prayer will call for you to formulate a prayer on the spot. But at other times there will be advance notice given and you will have the chance to prepare your words and phrases with more deliberation. Being asked to be worship leader on Laity Sunday, for example, will guarantee your preparation time. When this is the case, your first question will be, Where do I begin? This will be especially true if this will be the first time you have been called to give worship leadership.

As you begin composing your prayer for public use, it is important to keep several concerns before you.

To begin, ask yourself, What is the occasion? The answer has direct impact on what your prayer is all about.

In some communities, it is the custom to have a prayer at the beginning of high school sporting events. Or some civic clubs open the meeting with prayer. Each of these events calls for a different approach to prayer just as the events differ widely. The opening invocation in a woman's group meeting in a home calls for a still different preparation, as would a prayer to be given in a hospital sickroom. An agency employing the handicapped in a large city regularly starts the workday with a short chapel service, and that calls for a prayer suitable for that specific occasion.

The event defines the subject, the length and the mood of your public prayer. Taking note of the uniqueness of the occasion helps you to be creative, and avoids the annoying repetition that is devastating to public prayer.

There is a beloved elder in a congregation who is noted for his loving, caring ways. He is also noted for having basically one prayer. No matter what the event, his communication with God is a minor variation of his one prayer. Members of his congregation can tell you in advance what he will say. His problem is that the dedicated churchman assumes that once a prayer is composed it can be used again and again. The result is that his prayer does not embody what the group needs.

It is a help to write the nature of the event as one way of avoiding hackneyed phrases and ideas. Public prayer is an act of creativity and there are ways in which the event itself starts your mind to thinking in new directions.

Next, ask yourself the question, Who can I assume will be present? In your imagination, envision the group as it probably will appear. Let their faces parade before your thinking, so that you renew your acquaintance with them and freshen your intuition about their individual needs. Make the mental suggestion that Jesus Christ is standing in their midst; for what would you ask him on their behalf?

You know, of course, that everyone needs wider dimensions to their lives. You are sure that some have moments to celebrate and you feel this calls for thanksgiving. You guess that others need special wisdom as they set out at the beginning of a new relationship. Others, you surmise, are facing times of decision about entering a new business, moving to a different community, or purchasing another home. You see that for some families the last child is on the verge of leaving home and the parents will be alone.

As might be suspected, each of the moments in life could be observed in a special gathering. It could be an anniversary, a housewarming, a wedding reception, or a going-away party. Or the church could be honoring a splendid couple who has given years of loving service through the congregation.

You as the prayer leader need to be sensitive about the occasion and you should be aware of the emotional impact of these major events in the lives of persons. Be alert to the feelings people share during these kinds of times. Be asking yourself what kinds of sensations they would want you to share with God. Are there apprehensions and fears or gratitude and joy? Your trying to probe the depths of persons' feelings in advance calls for your best efforts at perception, but it will be well worth the energy when persons reflect with gratitude what your prayer means to them.

As you seek to put yourself in the mood of a group yet unformed, it would be good for you to have pencil and paper handy to jot down impressions as they come to you. Later these written impressions can be a part of the glue that cements the prayer together into a whole.

Another important consideration is the type of prayer you are asked to lead. Remember the worship service of the church where you attend. You recall that there are a number of prayers in the order of worship and that they vary in length and purpose.

Sometimes the order of worship is arranged around a particular religious observance. Those churches that closely follow a liturgical calendar often celebrate the day of a saint, and the prayers and sermon are arranged to help the congregation learn the outstanding qualities of the saint's life. It may be that the congregation is observing a special day of the church year, such as Pentecost, the "birthday of the church."

If you belong to one of the churches that does not follow the liturgical calendar, you may still observe that all the parts of your worship service are arranged to make a whole or total experience. Your pastor may have a general worship theme in mind and the prayers follow that topic. Sometimes the theme of the day is printed in the worship folder and this is a key to understanding the unity of the prayers and other elements of worship. With a little practice you can develop the ability to recognize how the service is unfolding about the theme and you can also become a worshiper who is participating more knowledgeably in the worship of the church.

Soon you will come to understand the critical importance of choosing and using the theme as a tool to keep your prayer from being fractured parts. As a prayer leader you will want to know what the worship service will have as the main subject. If it will be Laity Sunday, you will want to use the theme of the ministry of the laypersons of the congregation. Labor Sunday's prayer will concentrate on the contributions made by the workers of our nation. You will need to focus on worship and what religious rites mean if a sanctuary is being dedicated, or Christian education if the building is to be used for classrooms. The intentional use of the occasion as your theme will keep your prayer on the subject and will keep you from drifting off into generalities.

It is good to be natural and not forced. As this is true in the use you make of voice and inflection, so it is also valid with the theme you select and the words you use to expand your topic. Of course, to stand in the presence of God brings a sense of awe. "Woe is me!" cried the prophet Isaiah when he saw the Lord in the temple. "For I am lost; for I am a man of unclean lips and I dwell in the midst of a people of unclean lips; for my eyes have seen the King, the Lord of hosts!" (Isaiah 6:5)

But when we think about it, isn't it true that we are always in God's presence? Isn't it so that we are surrounded by him at all times? Though our awareness of him lacks the drama of the prophet's experience is he any less with us? Because God and we are constantly interacting, we should never assume that conversation with God must be marked by unusual words or phrases. We do not want to be casual in our friendship with God nor do we want to adopt a false formality. We need a style of prayer that is comfortable and fitting to our understanding of God's closeness and of his relationship to us.

For some, the question of style will also raise the question of whether public prayers should be written. Should the leader have the prayer written on a card to be carried into the chancel? Or should the leader attempt to memorize the prayer and recite it at the proper time? Would it be better to form only ideas in prior preparation and then "compose" the prayer extemporaneously at worship time? What is the best method and which should the leader choose? In some congregations a leader can be tugged in several directions.

There are those who feel that the best prayer "comes from the heart." By this they mean that a good prayer is one that is composed on the spot and made up as the conversation with God progresses. They suggest that to prepare a prayer in advance and to put it on paper makes for artificiality and tends to make the prayer more of a literary work than a prayer of the people of God. Moreover, extemporaneous prayer avoids the stiffness and formality that may be present with the written prayer. Unwritten prayers can better catch the moving of the Spirit of God and be sensitive to persons' needs at the time of prayer, they say. By being more spontaneous one really matches the prayer to the event of the day and lessens the guesswork about the mood of the worshipers, they feel. Real, effective prayer is that which is delivered without written guidance.

There are those who have such sensitivity and ability that they are able to compose a prayer in the instant and have the congregation feel warmth and power. It is as though there is a reservoir of prayer life on which they can draw and find new and fresh means of leading the family talk we know as prayer. Versed in language, experienced in leadership, and knowing the heart of the congregation, these great pray-ers are able by the richness of their words to God to lead us to know he is close. They lift the expectation that God will speak because he is so near.

While some churches are blessed with such leaders, other men and women feel that such an approach to public prayer is unnatural for them. The thought of going to lectern, altar, or table with little or nothing written leaves them with a bad case of hives!

The basic rule is to lead in a way that enables you to be a good steward of your ability. Having or not having a written prayer is neither good or bad. What is crucial is that you go to your post prepared and competent to lead.

Some who believe in spontaneous prayer should use a tape recorder to check for repetition and the length of their prayer. On some occasions, "Please lead us in prayer" means that the person leads and continues to lead past the point of having anything to say. Some leaders convey the impression that they think long rambling prayers are to be admired for their spontaneity. They should learn that this extreme in prayer is embarrassing to thoughtful persons who know prayer is not a protracted speech or oratorical demonstration.

The tape recorder can help those who write their prayers, too. Some prayers are obvious by being read instead of really prayed. Devoid of feeling, some written prayers are delivered with a wooden feeling and a mechanical mood. There is not much to commend this style either!

There is a man who, when asked to lead in prayer without advance notice, will refuse. He is not trying to be difficult. But he feels that prayer is too important a matter to be left to the invention of the moment and that the issues we face with God are so significant that only careful preparation can enable one to lead properly.

Perhaps that is going to an extreme, but it is true that prayer deals with concerns that are so important to people that the time must be used wisely. Preparation is necessary whether the prayer is written or not.

Even for spontaneous prayers, there is help in preparation. For one thing, leading in public prayer is eased when we feel comfortable with prayer in our private devotional life. If we are not in the custom of forming conversation with God in the privacy of a quiet room, on a walk through a forest, or in a place of secluded meditation, we probably are not comfortable in seeking to lead others in public prayer. When you are alone, do not hesitate to talk to God aloud. Become accustomed to the sound of your voice addressing God.

Another helpful method is to develop the habit of estimating the group as you enter. Size up what is happening. This is an asset in understanding the dynamics of the group as it functions; it is another way to prepare for spontaneous prayer. Usually you unconsciously note certain features of a group upon arrival. Obviously you see who is there. That may remind you of friendships or resentments from the past among members. You will determine whether people are enjoying themselves in conversation or whether there are certain ones standing alone and unnoticed. Ordinarily you will come with some understanding of why the meeting is being held. Sometimes you are able to perceive the morale of those who are there. By making careful mental notes of these signs you become a better member of the group and are more sensitive. It also helps you formulate a more relevant prayer if you lead one.

If you write your prayer and are using cards or a paper, you need to be discreet about handling the pages. Getting ready to participate in morning worship leadership means getting your materials in place for use. Before the service begins, place your materials at the lectern or pulpit. Have your papers in the order of their use to eliminate unnecessary shuffling and to make your leadership smoother. You can feel more comfortable knowing that you have things well in hand, and you communicate this to the congregation when the service starts.

The leader who uses a written prayer can lead with eyes partially closed and can avoid the appearance of reading a manuscript. Leaders serve best when they remember not to call attention to themselves. When the leader places the written prayer in the lectern, he or she should check to see if the words are at the proper distance to be seen without squinting and should use the time before the event to become familiar with the setting and arrangements.

Experiment with whether writing prayers is the style for you. Whatever inhibits your ability to guide the congregation in prayer should be changed to that which enhances your leadership.

This is a time of transition and modernization. No matter how comfortable or habitual a pattern or practice is, questions arise about new ways of doing things, and different approaches to old customs. This certainly is true in the forms of English that are used in prayer today. Conversational English is quickly replacing the Old English forms that reflect usage going back to pre-Shakespearean times. Because the transition is not yet complete, it is not uncommon to encounter both modern forms and the Old English being used in the same worship service and sometimes in the same prayer.

The Old English is easily recognized as sounding like the English of the King James version of the Bible. It embodies a language style noted for its grace and beauty and which is often identified as "religious language." Instead of "you," "thou" is used. "Are" is "art," "your" is "thy" or "thine." The criticism of this form of language is that persons simply do not talk this way in the modern world. Why does prayer call for this special way of speaking? Is not the divine ear able to hear the plain everyday language of the world? Does usage of such an old form of speech suggest that the worship and life of the church belong to a by-gone time?

There are some aspects of these questions you need to weigh as you form your public prayer style and adopt a language of prayer. With which do you feel more comfortable, the Old English or the modern forms? If you are not at ease with the language, your prayer will sound strained and you soon notice an unnatural quality to your leading. And of course you need to question if members of the congregation feel one form of language opens or closes doors to God.

One final inquiry of yourself is, do you really know how to use the Old English? If you are unfamiliar with the proper use of such classic forms you should use language that you clearly understand and which poses no uncertainties for you.

Whatever your decision about language forms, do not mix the modern and Old English in the same prayer. Be consistent. Follow one pattern throughout lest the shifting back and forth becomes a distraction to those who hear the obvious differences. You do not want your people paying more attention to the language than to the prayer.

The use of modern language does not mean, however, that it is appropriate to use slang in prayer. The exception to this can sometimes be found in certain situations such as one in which a minister was called to lead Sunday night services at a rescue mission downtown in a large city! In that particular setting, the minister felt the Sunday evening congregation of down-and-outers needed language with which they could more readily identify. While he was careful in what he said, his prayer language was far different from that of his Sunday morning worship.

There are exceptions, but in general, avoid slang. While terms such as "nitty-gritty" and "the bottom line" and "opening a can of worms" are familiar, they are used so much that they actually say little. Slang gives prayer a casualness that adds nothing and takes away a good deal. Carelessness with language conveys the impression that God is a pal or buddy with whom his people have not talked for awhile. It implies a chattiness that is foreign to good public prayer and casts a shadow over the majesty of God.

Let your prayers convey reverence for God, a sense of his awesomeness, and an awareness of his holiness which can, at best, be understood only partially.

A model for this is a walk through some of the Psalms and a look at how God is viewed. At no point is there the impression that God is anyone less than the Holy One of Israel, who hears and acts with might, compassion and wisdom. Psalm 10 is one of these. Here is a prayer where God is questioned, yet affirmed as the One who redeems the poor and downtrodden.

> Why dost thou stand afar off,
>    O LORD?
> Why dost thou hide thyself in times
>    of trouble? (vs. 1)

Here is the cry of one who has watched the tyrants of the earth oppress the people and who wants God to execute justice. But in his questioning, the Psalmist never denies that God is the One who has the power and majesty to effect that judgment. He concludes,

> O LORD, thou wilt hear the desire of the meek;
>    thou wilt strengthen their heart,
>       thou wilt incline thy ear
> to do justice to the fatherless and the
>       oppressed,
>    so that man who is of the earth
>       may strike terror no more. (vss. 17-18)

As you stroll through the Psalms you see that there is reverence in the midst of questions, faith in the middle of fear, and hope in the center of confusion. Without being stilted you can use language that portrays God's friendship at the heart of his majesty.

It is sometimes good to take a closer look at language that is being used to see if there are hidden things being taught.

One minister was pulled up short by a question from a woman who asked, "Why do you always use the term 'Father' in your prayers? Aren't there other terms with which to address God?" The pastor had not been aware that his language was conveying to her that her minister considered God as solely masculine. His parishioner was coming to God from a feminine perspective and she did not find that aspect of God's nature expressed in her pastor's prayers.

The use of non-sexist language is complicated by the fact that the Judeo-Christian tradition and history is that of a male-oriented society. In the Old and New Testaments, God is addressed as being masculine. The pastor who emphasized "Father" in his prayer follows a long line of those who use the masculine gender regarding God. For the modern church person, using new expressions of God's qualities offers both the opportunity to express the worth of all persons and the chance to make new discoveries about the vastness of God.

# ADDITIONAL PRAYERS

## For an anniversary of a couple in the church

OUR HOLY and loving Father, we thank thee for the joy of this moment as we share together this anniversary as friends and family. For the long years of life together which have grown and flourished because they were cultivated with love and patience, we thank thee. For the constancy that has enabled this couple to be strong in the face of difficulty and change, we thank thee. And for the growth in grace that each has experienced and shared with us, we give thee our thanks.

Wilt thou continue to make their lives radiant and so share thyself with us through them? Wilt thou open the doors of the future to them with the excitement of the past so they may move on to each new phase with that same fascination with what may be? In all thy gifts to them and to us, we praise thee, through Jesus Christ, Amen.

## For an anniversary of the church

O GOD of all time, of things seen and unseen, what feelings are in our hearts at this time! We have been privileged to pass one of those great milestones in the life of the church that remind us we are your people and the people you have chosen to fulfill your will and purpose. We have watched as the sacrifices of the past have been realized in the accomplishments of the present. We stand transfixed by a growing excitement of what can happen in the future by your power at work in us.

We pause to thank you for those who have been the pioneers, whose labors we have enjoyed and from whose vision we have profited. Like master craftsmen, they laid sound foundations and we have sought to build wisely upon that base. They gave time and money without regret and poured their energy into this church without regard for self. Enable us today to be so generous with what has been given to us, that following generations might know you.

For the accomplishments of this church, we rejoice. Imperfect, like all institutions, yet this church strives to be obedient, attempts to lift up the high and holy, the sacred and the noble.

Give, then, O God, the vision the leaders need for future growth and development. Supply them with the courage they need and the daring they must have to provide the guidance called for in these times. Help us to care for the sick, for those who do not know Christ, for the spiritually lost, and we shall seek to be faithful. Help us to nurture and teach all who come to find meaning and purpose to their lives, and we shall do our best. Help us to be a body of people who care about each other, and who care about those who are not of this circle. Help us to be the body of Christ at work in the world, through our Lord, Amen.

## For a meeting of the board, vestry, council, of the congregation

YOU, O God, have chosen some to be leaders, and have placed on their shoulders the burden and opportunity to help guide the church on its way in your mission. Dealing with sacred ideals, we are nonetheless human and so aware of how awesome is our responsibility in the offices you have given us. We are not clearly convinced you have chosen the right ones for the task, yet here we are, confronted with the business of your Kingdom.

How much we need logic and reasoning that will mean our judgments are made with coolness of deliberation! How much also we need that rare intuition that will help us sense what is good in the surprise of our interacting together! Each word from those around us calls for us to analyze our own thoughts; we need to develop in our ability to discern what Christ would have us do.

Help us to walk with him that as we share in this meeting, we will come to know his will; in his name, Amen.

## For a Sunday school class

O MASTER Teacher, open our minds that during this time together we might see new visions of truth. Where there are shadows, and understanding does not prevail, help us through the light of the teaching of Scripture to see you and your wisdom. We want our fellowship to be an experience of learning as we share our lives with each other. So banish closed minds and bias from our thinking. Keep us ever open to fresh and new awareness of the meaning and purpose of our lives. Before our expectant searching spring exciting discoveries for us, and so may we grow in wisdom and spiritual stature, through him who came teaching, Amen.

## For the birth of a child

OUR heavenly Father, our hearts burst with joy at the birth of (name) with whom you have blessed this family. We are reminded of the birth of Christ in the birth of each child; may this child grow as Jesus did to live a life that will praise and honor you. For the safekeeping of this mother, we give thanks as we offer our hopes in this new expression of life, through Jesus Christ, Amen.

O

## For an annual meeting of the congregation

O GOD, who is known as the God of action, for this year past we give thanks. More than the passage of time alone, the annual meeting represents the ministries of the church as it seeks to reach out, and we thank you where we have been fruitful. We look at what we as your family have done, and evaluate the work with the hope that the next year will bring greater effort, better investment of your money, and working even closer in harmony with your purposes for this congregation.

We are thankful for the loyalty of our members and friends, and for the selfless giving that enables the work to be done. The willingness to be used in your service makes our labor together happy.

We thank you for the newcomers to our fellowship, for the new members who have come to confess the Christ as Lord, for the children born into the family of the church, and for those who have been drawn by the irresistible love of Christ as expressed by persons.

We are saddened by the loss of those who have died or moved away. Yet we rejoice even in sorrow by the ties of Christian love that remind us that neither distance nor death have power finally to separate.

Crown this coming year then with new hope, creative plans, vital energy, deepened commitment, and above all, your favor on our work for you. We pray in the name of Jesus Christ, Amen.

O

## For the dedication of children

O GOD, whose Son beckoned the little children that they come to him, we come this day as congregation, parents, and sponsors to present to you (these children/ this child) for dedication. Will you bless (them/ him/ her) by unfolding before (them/ him/ her) the plan of life that leads to full and rich living as we have come to know life in Christ?

As parents, we come asking for the wisdom and knowledge that will enable us to guide our children (our child) and to maintain a home where there is noble and unselfish devotion to goodness and truth. Help us to be good teachers of those values that Christ taught which are childlike in their beauty, purity, and righteousness. May our children (our child) come to understand that the love we share in our families (family) is an extension of that divine love you have for us.

As a congregation, inspire us to work for a world where children can grow and flourish and where hate is banished. Help us to teach those things that make for life, and to be fearless in our denunciation of that which makes for wrong. In all our dealings with one another and with the world, remind us that we are Christ in the world, his body, and so we are teachers by deed and word.

In this moment of dedication, may our vows and pledges be made in firmness and fidelity that these children (this child) will grow to be your servants (servant) like Christ, Amen.

## For the world mission of the church

O GOD, who sent your followers out into the world, beginning in Jerusalem and going to all people with the Good News, empower us to catch a glimpse of that same vision that thrust early disciples out and launched the mission of the church for all time.

We thank you for those whose lives are dedicated to the holy cause of spreading the gospel of Jesus Christ through their words and talents. Doctors and nurses, agricultural technicians, and teachers, all go about their tasks helping tell the story of Christ and his caring. Pastors and administrators, builders and craftsmen portray the loving Lord in daily work.

Help us who do not go to far scenes to work to remember those whom we send out in the name of Christ. May they know of our concern for them and their work. May our support of their efforts sustain and uphold them in moments of discouragement. When night falls and the human spirit sags with fatigue, may our love bridge the miles of separation to renew tired minds with thoughts of friends who share the same faith.

Stir our hearts and wills, O God of all people, that we will be generous with what we have to offer and so, through our gifts, be a part of that which we cannot do personally. Place the world mission of the church before us, and challenge us, we pray in the name of him who sent his followers out, Jesus Christ, Amen.

O

## A prayer for a minister to use at the beginning of a new day

FATHER GOD, I your servant face all the promise of a new day, given to me as a trust. Keep me faithful in my task, always keeping before my mind the thought of Christ and his ministry. I want to be holy and wise, pure and clean, loving and compassionate in all my dealings with those whom I shall meet this day. Lead me not into the temptation to think more highly of myself than I ought, nor to become confused about who comes first. Remind me that I preach the gospel in committee meetings as much as from the pulpit, and proclaim Christ as I talk with someone who is wounded by life as much as in a formal sermon. Use all that I have to offer you, O God, in ways that are pleasing to you. Through Jesus Christ, Amen.

## A prayer for a minister to use at the end of the day

HOLY SPIRIT of God, I give back to you this day of service, used to your glory. There were problems that remain unsolved, and I place them in your hands. Many needs were unmet and I must give them to you as well. But this day's work has also brought victories for Christ, and we celebrate what you have done.

Forgive me for the mistakes that pressure and haste have created, and for the impatience and frustration that made me rush through relationships too hurriedly.

Renew me with the dawn for a fresh day's work, to pick up the task again, and to be faithful. In Christ's name, Amen.

## A prayer for a fellowship dinner

DEAR GOD, we gather together as the church to share our lives in Christian friendship as we have this meal today. By our eating as one people we proclaim to all that we are united, and have food as one family. May the food that we distribute be as the bread and wine of the communion. Remind us you are in our midst and are known in our breaking of bread. Shine in the radiance of the meeting of new friends and the sealing of new affection for each other.

Help us to learn from the program of the evening; open to our minds new aspects of your truth and make us ever ready to be about your work. Through Jesus Christ, our Lord, Amen.

# CHAPTER 3

SOME TYPES OF PUBLIC PRAYERS
Prayers in the public worship service
Prayers for other occasions

IN MOST worship services, the public prayers tend to follow the psychological progression of the order. That is, moods and feelings change as the service unfolds as in any public event.

First, we come with a sense of reverence as we first approach God. We are struck by the quiet mood of the sanctuary in the early moments which reminds us of the dimensions and nature of God. We kneel or sit in awe of the One who is holy and lifted up. We experience calls to worship, stirring processional hymns and words of worship which help us ponder the God who holds all things in hand.

Second, we find ourselves in the atmosphere of fellowship, not with our neighbors, but with God. This feeling of oneness with him is inspired by the reading of scripture and the pastoral prayer.

After the time of fellowship with him, we want to do something that symbolizes our love and oneness with God. So we are stirred by a spirit of dedication in which we make an offering or expression of devotion.

As powerful as this sense of dedication is, the movement of renewal sweeps in and the mood of empowerment takes over to send the church out into the world to be God's servants in love and service. The renewal is often characterized by the celebration of the Lord's Supper or communion.

This is the way worshipers move mentally and emotionally through the day's worship. They come as searchers; they are rekindled for life's demands. It is important to be aware of this movement because the prayers in many church services are based on this progression and are arranged to be a part of a progressive pattern.

Let's look at each of these movements again in order:


REVERENCE →FELLOWSHIP
↘
DEDICATION →RENEWAL


In the bulletin there sometimes are variations where one act of worship may be combined with the one that follows. The basic pattern, however, is that of searchers coming to find, and finding, they give. And in giving they receive orders to go out and are sent forth with new vision and hope.

# THE INVOCATION

Often the first prayer is the invocation. It is in the time of reverence. This prayer is relatively short and asks God to make the congregation aware of his abiding and constant presence.

The word "invoke" means "to call," but it is important to understand that this means to call *on* God rather than to beckon to him. The invocation thus turns the attention of the people to God in the initial moment and sets the stage for what follows.

It is a natural temptation to ask God to "be with us." But a look behind such a petition shows a presumption that he is somehow away and comes back on occasion. Perhaps there is to be another absence after the worship and God needs to be recalled! The invocation appears to be used as just such a summons on some occasions and often seems to be teaching that God does come and go. Nothing could be further from the truth! If God seems far away it is caused by human indifference and preoccupation, not divine geography! The invocation needs to call for the awareness of the people to what already is.

Your remembering that the central purpose of the invocation is to ask God to sharpen the spiritual senses of the congregation guarantees that you do not get involved in unimportant matters in the opening prayer. When you compose an invocation it would be good for you to jot down the purpose in your own words. Later look at the finalized version to see whether your composition keeps the central purpose intact. Do you ask God to enable the congregation to discover him, and do you seek God's help in turning to him? If so, then the chances are the congregation will feel this during the worship hour.

Let's look at some model invocations. You might want to try these as they are, or you could use them as examples for composing your own invocations.

OUR LORD, who constantly shines with truth and peace, radiate light into our lives this hour and lift our spirits that we might turn to those things that are high and holy and so be known as the sons and daughters of the Most High. In Jesus' name, Amen.

ETERNAL ONE, whose love is beyond compare and whose forgiveness is without measure, make us pure and holy of heart, strong and valiant servants, with keen minds and ready hands, quick to do thy will, we ask in Jesus' name, Amen.

O GOD, we come expectantly awaiting the revealing of yourself, and sensitive to your presence in word and the deeds of the church; during this hour of worship, may our lips praise you, may our songs glorify you, and may our lives be turned to you, the Source of all light, in the spirit of Jesus Christ, Amen.

OUR GOD and Father of the Babe in the manger, in this Christmas season you bring again the news that thrills the world, that the Christ is born; grant that he might be born in each heart today; open our ears to hear the glad songs again, and fill our lives with the peace that he came to bring, through Jesus Christ our Lord, Amen.

O GOD who hast taught us that those who build do so in vain unless thou art the real designer; create within us this day of dedication a new vision of teaching, a fresh understanding of the educational task of the church, and a renewed commitment to help children grow "in wisdom and in stature, and in favor with God and man," Amen.

Consider how each of these invocations, some for special events, keeps central the God who comes and reveals himself. These prayers are brief, direct, and do not stray from the desire to be led into a new experience of awareness and service.

# PASTORAL PRAYERS

The prayer that is probably the most widely recognized is the pastoral prayer. It is longer, for one thing, and includes more diverse elements for another. Because the pastoral prayer contains more parts and addresses a broader expanse of needs, the pastoral prayer is likely to be identified as "the prayer" of the morning. And because of its unique role in the life of the church and the needs of its members, a special look needs to be taken at the pastoral prayer.

The name of the prayer provides an interesting study. It might be thought from a casual look that the name implies that it is the prayer of the pastor. In most cases it is the minister, priest, or pastor who delivers the pastoral prayer except on those days that call for lay participation. Even then it is not unusual for the pastoral prayer to be reserved for the clergy with lay persons taking other roles in the worship, including the sermon.

However, instead of identifying the pastoral prayer with the person who leads it, it is better to look at the content to see why it is called the "pastoral" prayer.

The pastoral prayer is so called because it includes those great pastoral needs of the church. That is, it is the prayer that brings before God the cares, hurts, hopes, and dreams of the people of the church. The feelings of the church are opened and set before the Good Shepherd. The term "pastoral" refers then to the nature of the Shepherd, God.

It is often thought that because of the intensity of this prayer and its priestly nature, the pastor is the one who should be the leader. However, anyone who has pastoral sensitivity could lead such a prayer, and many lay leaders have developed the capacity to lead the congregation in pastoral prayers that are both touching and expressive.

It is an aid to see an old acrostic that will help in remembering the parts of a pastoral prayer.

A—ADORATION
C—CONFESSION
T—THANKSGIVING
S—SUPPLICATION
S—SURRENDER

ACTSS is a tool that can be used in seeing that pastoral prayers includes those aspects of the Christian life that the congregation needs. Not every pastoral prayer will include each of these elements every time, but often they are all present in the pastoral prayers of worship services.

The pastoral prayer comes at the time of fellowship because the sharing is with God instead of a time of talking to neighbors. The reading of the Scriptures is accompanied by the pastoral prayer when the congregation talks with God. The will of God is made known in the reading of the Bible; now there is a chance to share with him in the words of the pastoral prayer.

One of the besetting dangers of the pastoral prayer is that it is easy to allow the prayer to become too long. Here is an experiment that will help you lead better. When the pastoral prayer begins at your morning worship service, make a note of the time. Follow the prayer carefully. If the leader finishes before your attention wanders, note the number of minutes the prayer took. If your mind strays before the prayer is concluded, look at the minutes it took before you drifted.

It is difficult to maintain concentrated prayer for more than three minutes. This may vary with individuals, but there are limits to the length of time intense prayer can be conducted without losing the congregation. The pastoral prayer is to be the prayer of the people, not the prayer of the leader. If the people have passed the point of concentration and are off chasing mental squirrels through the trees, the pastoral prayer is no longer the church's voice. A prayer that is too long and which seeks to include every item under the sun will soon lose the persons who are to benefit from the prayer.

Here are some prayers that are pastoral in nature and which seek to embody adoration, confession, thanksgiving, supplication, and surrender.

47

OUR FATHER, who art the Father of us all; we bring the poverty of our lives to the richness of Christian worship and adoration. Every day bursts with the splendor of thy glory; the whole earth is filled with the signs of thy passing. Thou hast touched our eyes and ears and minds till we are sure thou art everywhere. In the order of law and nature we know thy care for us; in the love of church and friends and familiar words of hymn and scripture we behold thy affection and saving mercy. In this instant we are thine and our love for thee defies any power to snatch us from thee.

How we would live better lives! How we would be more forgiving, less critical. How we need thee, O Father, to make friends instead of enemies, and by an encouraging word of understanding seek to exert the magnetic pull of divine love. Judge our failures and shortcomings and inadequacies, O Lord, where we can clearly see what should be in their place. Save us from the feeling of having arrived, but keep us ever working at the business of building a life. And teach us to construct wisely so we are not making something of shoddy materials or building with the sand of falsehood. Help us to be honest with ourselves.

Our age, O God, needs peacemakers so much. Help all persons to learn the blessings of peace and the folly of war. Create a new world where righteousness, justice and peace will not be simply words, but realities.

For the sick and distressed wilt thou make them conscious of thy sustaining presence? Because they are in our circle of love, we unite our thoughts and hopes with theirs. Help them through the services others render to them. Draw them close to all who have shared in human suffering, yet who also have known divine strength.

Help us, too, Lord, to find our place for adequate service. Show us how we best can use our time and talents for thee. Give us jobs that draw from us our best, for that is what we offer thee in love and worship, through Jesus Christ, Amen.

Here is another pastoral prayer that was offered before a congregation where the pastor knew of several who were wrestling with whether they could function in a time of religious and civil controversy. In addition to the sermon which sought to deal with the turbulent times, he led the congregation in this prayer.

OUR GOD of all time, the glory of your presence is ever before us. The coming of the dawn, the changing seasons, the unfolding of your creation all serve to remind us of your beauty. We have seen you in peace and we have known you in time of trouble that rages and threatens. We look, and you are everywhere, often in the strangest places. We have heard you speak in Jesus Christ as we have never heard you speak before, through a carpenter who took us so poor in soul and who made us rich indeed!

Deliver us from lostness, from the willful pride that keeps us from hearing the call of conscience. Save us from being self-appointed critics of our neighbors.

Save us, O Lord, from the violence that leads our world into seeking solutions by force rather than by righteousness and truth. Touch those who would enslave persons that they might set others free instead.

Anxieties plague us, Father. Set us loose from the worries about money, our health or social position. Keep us from feeling sorry for ourselves in whatever place we are found.

Make us strong mentally, physically, and spiritually so that we can be Christlike in our lives, in what we think and do. Help us to be good stewards and good workers where we are called. Help us to do our best, for what else can we give to you? Do with us what we need, make us what we ought to be.

We give our lives to you in humble service. Keep our promise to you fresh in our minds and ever before us as we speak and act. Where we fall, restore us, and use us wherever you wish. In Jesus' name, Amen.

The pastoral prayer that is able to capture expression of the hurts and needs will be rewarded with gratitude. The pastoral prayer, of course, is not the place for preaching, and good taste requires that the prayer be worded in such a way that no one is embarrassed. Prayer is therapy, not confrontation or a place to argue a point.

## THE OFFERTORY PRAYER

In most churches the offertory prayer comes during the time of dedication. The purpose of the offertory prayer is to express the thanksgiving of the membership for the material possessions and the spirit that make the offering possible. It is also to affirm to God the desire that the gifts placed in loving service on the altar will be used and multiplied by God.

Because the nature of the offertory prayer is one of thanksgiving and dedication, the prayer comes after the offering is received from the people. A part of this is the practical matter that there is a temptation to pray that the people be generous! But the prayer comes after the offering for a more important reason.

The offering is far more than the way the church finances its operation. It is true that most of the money received by the church comes in this fashion, but it is a mistake to assume that the budget is the real and most significant meaning of the offering! Actually, the offering is one of the ways the church expresses devotion. It is a tangible means of communicating concern for the causes of God. Therefore, the offertory prayer speaks of the gratitude of the people and of the desire to share as a display of thanksgiving. There is a vibrant hope that the gifts are acceptable. The size and amount of the offering varies from church to church, but there is a similar hope that motivates the offertory prayer in all congregations.

In some worship services the offertory prayer is offered immediately after the offering is brought forward during the singing of the Doxology. Custom varies regarding where the offering is received or the location from which the offertory prayer is given.

The thinking of church members about money can be interesting and often filters over into the content of the offertory prayer. There is still a persistent belief that righteousness and prosperity are somehow connected and that poverty and evil are linked in some way. Others turn this around and link wealth and wickedness. How this is viewed varies from church to church, observed one who felt a church's perspective of wealth depended on whether it was a rich or a poor church!

We do have to be careful of such assumptions when we lead the offertory prayer. We give of our financial resources for a variety of reasons. These are the material things we offer for the service of the kingdom of God. The capacity to use these gifts can be increased more than is dreamed possible.

However, the offertory prayer is a chance to lift up the hope of the Christian that all might elude the self-centeredness that causes vanity and indulgence. Therefore, the offertory prayer can express the awareness that all gifts come from God and that these gifts are a trust. As an act of dedication the offertory prayer provides the opportunity to focus on the self-giving nature of God and frames a verbal response to that holy gift.

O GOD, you are the giver of every good and perfect gift; we seek to return a portion of these things you have bestowed upon us to be invested and used wisely in your service. Conscious of your self-giving, we would try to be self-givers, too. Enable us more and more to be like the Christ who is the example of what a servant is. It is our hope that this offering will be a worthy symbol of our devotion to you. Please accept these offerings as tokens of our lives offered to you, in the name of Jesus Christ, Amen.

OUR heavenly Father, who has looked on the world created full and good, we are not our own but we belong to you. Nothing that we have comes to us except that it came from you. While we have labored, you have given the growth and life. So our offering is tarnished unless we give from the generosity that springs from love for you. As bread and fish were multiplied by our Lord, take these offerings and supply the wants and needs of a multitude, we ask in Christ, Amen.

O GOD of our lives, we dedicate these offerings in the hope that they will be a part of the great offering and outpouring of your church that will bring healing and hope to our land and world. Bind up the wounded and heal the brokenhearted and by your work and word bring peace and unity to all people, through Jesus Christ, Amen.

## COMMUNION PRAYERS

The calling for communion prayers varies greatly from denomination to denomination. In some churches the option for lay leadership in the Lord's Supper may be very limited or non-existent.

Some denominations have the practice of using lay leaders for the prayers, while the words of institution are spoken by the minister. Some congregations observe the Lord's Supper with no ministerial participation in the ritual.

Ordinarily, for those churches where the observance is weekly, the communion is shared during the time of renewal. It may come before the sermon in some cases. Others have the Lord's Supper as the last act of worship, seeing the breaking of bread and the drinking of the cup as the final empowerment before the church goes into the world to serve.

The interpretation of this event and the meaning the denomination places on the Lord's Supper certainly has an impact on the content of the communion prayer.

Most Protestants feel that the bread and wine are symbols of the body and blood of Christ. Hence, while the elements are viewed with respect, the bread and cup are not in any sense seen as the actual physical being of Jesus Christ. Roman Catholics feel that at the moment of consecration the wafer and wine actually become Christ's body and blood.

From time to time, the prayers at the altar or communion table reflect a theological position which is not held by the denomination or the congregation. If there are questions in this regard it would be good for an appointment to be made with the pastor to get information on matters of interpretation.

Because we are a people who are crossing denominational lines when we move from community to community, we regularly find ourselves participating in a church other than the one with which we are familiar. Therefore we need to take time to grow in our understanding of the new tradition where we are participating and we ought to be prepared to do the study necessary to appreciate its history and thought.

In many churches there are two prayers at the communion table, one for the bread and one for the cup. It is often the custom for the bread to be consecrated and distributed for participation, then the same process is repeated for the cup. Sometimes both bread and wine are distributed together, but there is prayer for each at the table. Other churches have only one prayer. A number of churches serve the communion by having the congregation file forward to the altar.

Here are some sample prayers, some for the bread and others for the wine.

O GOD, we humbly come before you, reminded in this bread of the body of our Lord Jesus Christ. As we share this loaf today, help us to acknowledge that we are his body in the world today. Take away our inclination to sin, and recreate us afresh and anew, Amen.

O LORD of life, to know you is never to thirst. As we look at the scarlet cup we ponder the meaning of the life of Jesus Christ, poured out for us. Will you bless us in this hour by helping us to walk more nearly in his way? Renew us for your purposes, we pray in Christ's name, Amen.

AS WE come to break bread together, O Lord, rekindle in our memories the thought of our Lord's self-giving. Eating of this bread nourishes both our bodies and our spirits as we rededicate our lives to him who is the Bread of Life. In the spirit of the Master, Amen.

JUST see how we come to you, O God, with our lives burdened with brokenness, to be refreshed about this sacred table. Consecrate for us this wine that as it becomes a part of us we shall become a part of you, Amen.

Communion prayers, like those for the offering, are short and direct. The prayers at the sacred table are not for the items individuals think should have been included in the pastoral prayer but weren't. Communion prayers are those of restoration, forgiveness and revival of Christian living. They center on the bread and wine, Jesus Christ and God's gift, as well as the call to join in holy and sacrificial living.

At times worshipers have been subjected to lengthy petitions relating to everything but the bread and wine. The members have breathed sighs of relief when the prayer was ended. And why not, for they came to that moment with the expectancy of meeting their Christ only to be turned aside. A clear mandate comes to leaders in the words of the Greeks who came to worship at the Passover, "Sir, we wish to see Jesus." (John 12:21)

## CLOSING PRAYERS

Many congregations close the worship with benedictions which are scriptual words and in a sense are not really in the same category as closing prayers. However, these scriptural words are said and given to the congregation in prayerful form. A couple are readily recognizable since they are used regularly.

MAY the God of steadfastness and encouragement grant you to live together in such harmony with one another, in accord with Christ Jesus, that together you may with one voice glorify the God and Father of our Lord Jesus Christ. (Romans 15:5-6)

MAY the peace of God, which passes all understanding, keep your hearts and minds in Christ Jesus. (Phil. 4:7 modified)

54

Some worship services close with ascriptions of praise such as the following:

NOW to him who by the power at work within us is able to do far more abundantly than all that we ask or think, to him be glory in the church and in Christ Jesus to all generations, for ever and ever. (Eph. 3:20-21)

TO THE King of ages, immortal, invisible, the only God, be honor and glory for ever and ever. (1 Tim. 1:17)

If the leader chooses a closing prayer rather than a benediction or ascription of praise, he or she will want to see that the prayer is a fitting climax to the worship and blends into what has gone before.

O GOD, we commit our lives to you even as we leave to seek to hasten the coming of your kingdom, that your will shall be done on earth as in heaven. In the name of Jesus, Amen.

O LORD of life, send us forth into the fray with renewed hearts and minds. It is good that we have been here, but we cannot stay. We must go from this sacred place to the world which is a sacred place, too, where persons need Jesus Christ and his healing hands. In his spirit, Amen.

# PRAYERS FOR OTHER OCCASIONS

It is a delight to have a chance to participate in worship that does not fit the pattern of the Sunday morning ritual.

On one occasion a church family asked the pastor to come to their new home and conduct a service of dedication for the house which they had just purchased. In one of those warm and rich events that happen along, the pastor found himself in the center of family worship that was intimate and where God seemed especially close.

Following the reading of scripture and a short meditation on the meaning of house and home, the minister led his small congregation in a prayer of blessing:

O THOU who art the head of every home and the foundation of every family that turns to thee, we give thee thanks for this new home and for the family that lives here. We rejoice in the sounds of laughter and joy and happiness, and celebrate with them this occasion when we can turn to thee and seek the warmth and radiance of thy presence. We thank thee for homes where the family can know love, affection, and mutual acceptance. A house which provides shelter from the storms of nature also helps protect us from the attacks of life and we can know peace in the midst of struggle. We are grateful for this. We hope for good things for this family in its future and ask that thou aid them in keeping faith strong and pure. All through Jesus Christ, Amen.

A number of civic clubs open their meetings with prayer. This can provide an opportunity to put to work the principles of preparation.

What is the makeup of the group? Who is there? Are there widely differing religious backgrounds of the members? Are there special needs any might be having? Does anyone appear perplexed or in any way apart from the group? Are some business people feeling particular pressures? Seeking answers to these questions will help the prayer that is given be more than simply a part of the opening exercise.

Here is a prayer that was offered by one member of the Rotary Club at one of its weekly meetings:

O GOD, we thank you for this meeting when we can come together as friends and share our lives and problems and opportunities. We come to learn to serve our community better, and we ask your help in our coming to understand how we can improve as citizens. Deepen our friendships and enable us to be helpers of one another through this organization and the relationships that we enjoy. Amen.

## TABLE GRACE

Table grace is public prayer. Sometimes abandoned in the hectic pace of modern living, the prayer before the meal can offer a time when the family is together in thought and word as well as in physical presence. Table grace does not have to be elaborate, but it ought to be a means of the family's saying thanks to God for the food and homes that it enjoys. In some families each person takes a turn at leading the grace. Hands may be joined around the table as the leader prays. Each member of the family grows quiet and thinks on the goodness of God in providing for them.

Table grace can be a good training spot for public prayer. It affords the chance to lead in a solid, secure situation which is known and non-threatening. Wise parents see this teaching opportunity and help their children grow accustomed to praying about the table. There is the danger, of course, that table prayers can be memorized and recited rather than prayed, but careful guidance by thoughtful adults can help the youngsters develop prayers that avoid repetition and simple ritualistic practice.

Prayers grow from understandings that are cultivated. Looking through books of prayers can help identify a variety of ways of expressing gratitude for meal and home. Here are some table graces that can be used to start the family in the practice of prayer at mealtime.

GOD of grace, we rejoice and give thanks to you for the bounty you have set before us, Amen.

**B**Y THIS food strengthen us to do your will and bless our service to you, for Christ, Amen.

**W**E THANK you with grateful hearts, O God, for these gifts you have given. Remind us of those who have no food and help us share with them, as with Jesus, Amen.

**E**VERYTHING points to your care for us, Father, and every gift speaks of your love for us. Humbly we accept this food as an expression of your care, through Jesus Christ, Amen.

**O** GOD, we thank you for this food and all the gifts that come our way. Enable us to live this day in such a way that we shall, in a small measure, be worthy of your grace, in Christ, Amen.

## BUILDING DEDICATIONS

One of the highlights in the life of any congregation is the dedication of a new building. Worship and education facilities are customarily consecrated for sacred use in a special service upon completion of construction. Architects, contractors, pastors, denominational representatives, and members of the congregation share in the celebration. During the service of dedication, prayers are often given by members of the church who are selected because of the role they have played in the building process, the office they hold, or the length of their membership in the church.

Buildings are offerings to God in service. They are not ends in themselves. They are means by which God shares himself, but buildings are not gods. Thus on this kind of occasion the prayer should be one of thanksgiving, hope that God will use the building to his glory, and a pledge on behalf of the congregation that it will do all it can to further the cause of God. The specific emphasis on dedication and the setting apart of the building provides the theme about which to compose the prayer. The following prayers can be used in a building dedication.

O YOU who are the Master Architect, yet who builds in life, we thank you for the meaning of this day as our dreams and labors come to completion. We are grateful for the work that made this building possible, for the consecrated persons who gave of their money and time and talents because of their commitment to your cause.

May this building now be dedicated to your service, and may its use always be to reflect glory and honor to your name. May it be a place of peace and hope, of growth and learning, and of spiritual refreshment and renewal.

Help us to whom it is entrusted to be good stewards in its use, caring for it as an investment in your work and making it a witness for your love and care, through Jesus Christ, Amen.

HEAVENLY God, who is pleased to give gifts to your people, we are indeed the recipients of a good gift in this building which we come to dedicate this day. We set it aside for your use, to be a house of worship and learning, where your praises are sung, and where your people can find a place of prayer in a world of tumult. We declare, Father, that this is a holy place, not that it can imprison your Spirit, but that we can find freedom from sin and brokenness through the gospel that is preached here and the sacraments that are observed here. Accept the offering of this house of worship, then, as a token of our love, in Christ, Amen.

# CHAPTER 4

ELEMENTS AND PARTS OF PUBLIC
PRAYERS
    Addressing God
    Dealing with human brokenness
    Gratitude
    Making "all my wants and wishes known"
    Giving us back to God
    The authority of Jesus

YOU WILL remember that earlier the acrostic ACTSS was used to keep before you the parts of the pastoral prayer. Actually every prayer will contain some of the elements:

A-Adoration
C-Confession
T-Thanksgiving
S-Supplication
S-Surrender

Having these five elements before you as you compose your public prayer will guide you in the formation of content so that your prayer will more nearly meet the spiritual needs of your members. In order for the congregation to have a well-rounded prayer life, it will need balanced expressions of these regularly.

The first words of prayer usually are those that address God. No salutation is exhaustive of God's nature, and thus there is unlimited opportunity for expressions of God's character. Many titles are used to describe God in prayer, and it is wise to vary the terms used to open the conversation with God. Many of these titles can come directly from Scripture and it is good to have the experience of the biblical people who share the fruits of the relationship with God. And, of course, newer expressions come as God is experienced by people in modern times.

The title with which we are the most familiar is simply "God." Along with that basic word we often put in some other phrase which we want to lift up as important in that moment. We find almost endless variations on this method of composing an address to God.

God of our fathers
God and Father of us all
God and Father of our Lord Jesus Christ
God of the universe
God of the atoms
God who touchest earth with beauty
God of grace and God of glory
Almighty God
God of life
    and so on.

God is often referred to as "Lord." This term comes from ancient times and reflects the fact that "lordship" is absolute in power and rule. The lord is a ruler. In the biblical image, he owns persons as slaves and has total control over their future and destiny. Persons owe utter obedience and loyalty to their lord. While there is a loving and caring mood when Christians use this term it is easy to see how the term "Lord" belongs to God.

The word "Father" was brought by Jesus into the thinking of persons of his time when they were considering God. "Father" in Jesus' time carried with it the idea of the head of the family. The father ruled the family. It was his wisdom that directed the activity of the members and it was he who made the crucial choices. "Father" did not carry the modern concept of family; he did not allow it to be even a semi-democracy.

God as Father was seen as caring and concerned almost beyond imagination, but also absolute in his demands for obedience. The Father was not harsh or cruel, but did anticipate the children's acceptance of his ways and will. He could be disobeyed, but the disobedience meant the choice to be separated from him and the family that he offers.

Experimenting with a list of various reverent addresses can build a reservoir of terms that can be used later and can help the congregation be exposed to new thoughts about the nature of God. The list might include such as these:

God, Sovereign Ruler, King, Eternal Friend, Master, Great Shepherd, Holy Parent, Governor of the Universe, Creator, Fountain of Life, and so on.


In some denominations where theology permits, prayers are addressed to Jesus Christ as though Jesus and God are the same. Other denominations' theological thinking indicates that God alone is to be addressed in prayer. A consultation with the pastor is helpful here to determine what is appropriate, and one's own feelings are important.

The beginning of the prayer opens the door to the first major component of public prayer: adoration. It is to God that glory and praise belong.

The earth is the LORD's and the fullness thereof, the world and those who dwell therein... (Ps. 24:1)

It is the act of adoration that we proclaim the glory of God. It is here that we share our sense of wonder, admiration, awe. Adoration turns us from the littleness of earth and its ways and problems. We concentrate instead on the majesty and greatness of God. In the act of adoration we direct the congregation toward the vastness of God's resources, knowledge and power. We try to help our people catch a glimpse of the adequacy and sufficiency of the Creator and Sustainer of the world. We share him who offers hope of salvation and deliverance from the perplexities of living.

O GOD, who dwells in the high and holy place and yet are with those who are humble of heart, we worship you. You have created the earth and the world; you have set the planets in their courses; and you have made all things good.

We stand in awe of the mighty power so displayed in the changing of the seasons, in the rain and snow that fall to nourish and water the earth. Holy, holy, holy, Lord God of hosts, the whole earth is full of your glory!

ETERNAL Father, gratefully we come to another day which you have made and crowned with glory because it is yours. We see your passing everywhere and we sense your presence in all that is. You are the great King, the ruler of the ends of the earth! You have no beginning and no end and all the nations of the earth owe homage and praise to you. We worship and praise your name.

**H**OLY, holy, holy, Lord God Almighty! Our words are inadequate to express our praise, yet our hearts cry out to you who are the Maker of all that is. From the smallest grain of sand to the far reaches of the universe, all things reflect the glory of our God. We stand blinded by your righteousness and splendor, lost in wonder, overwhelmed by your love, and mastered by your will.

**T**O you, O God, be all praise and glory! From the rising of the sun, through the noon to the coming of night, may your name be praised! Your deeds are greater than we can comprehend, your love more than we can understand. The vastness of your forgiveness! We scarcely can believe it! How great you are and how wonderful! To you be all praise and glory, for ever and ever!

We feel a need for confession when we realize, standing before God's goodness, how unhappy and distressed we are. We become acutely aware how our lives are marred with sin and disobedience. We are reminded by words of scripture, such as Romans 2 and 3, that sin is no respecter of persons. No matter who we are, despite all external appearances, we have all felt the jarring of sin.

The apostle Paul makes the case that forgiveness is available as a gift but the gift must be received by those who are ready to obtain it. Confession is that act by which the offer becomes ours as we acknowledge neediness and an openness to receive forgiveness.

**W**E COME sorry for the wrongs we have done, for the moments of life spent unwisely, for the hot and hasty words that have brought pain and distress to others, and for our self-centeredness that has kept us from hearing the truth spoken in love by our friends. If we have offended you, O God, or inflicted suffering to neighbor, please forgive.

O

**F**ORGIVE US, O God, for we have walked in the ways of brokenness. The good we wanted to do seemed so difficult and the evil we wanted to shun seemed so easy. Apathy robbed our strength and we wanted to be as others, so in moments of weakness we succumbed and fell from what you wanted.

**O** GOD, how little our lives have become when we wanted to enlarge and expand them! We became absorbed in our own needs and forgot the needs of others. We walked in our own world of plenty and dismissed those who had not. We were deaf to the calls of the hurt, for we were too busy satisfying our appetites. We defaced your image in us by not caring. Forgive us, we ask, and lead us to the larger life.

**W**E SEEK forgiveness, O God, for the wrongs with which we have afflicted friends and neighbors. We seek forgiveness for the wrongs committed against you in the deeper recesses of our minds. Forgive us for being unwilling to bend to your loving kindness. We have put our opinions before your word. Stubbornly, we have sought our own way, and kept you out.

Once we speak the words that describe our guilt we are ready to experience forgiveness and are moved to thanksgiving. For all God's gifts we should be thankful. The creation, our families, homes, jobs, and nation are all reasons we should have grateful minds when we come to worship. But as valuable as all these are, what greater gift could we have than Jesus Christ? It is he who makes sense out of living. It is he who liberates us from the clutches of sin and death and provides us with the clearest vision of God. Do you see why confession has to open us to thanksgiving as we become aware that it is for us that Christ died? We are set free! So while we are thankful for the good things we enjoy, the most prominent favor for which we want to voice indebtedness is Jesus Christ. The material possessions, food, clothing, and all else, are expressions of the divine love that was made flesh in Christ. As we express gratitude for those things we are also touched by the fact that they point to the supreme demonstration of God's love in the life and ministry of the Carpenter of Nazareth.

Sometimes it helps to be more intentional about our giving of thanks. A kind of "thanks inventory" needs to be taken occasionally as we need to be looking at items in life for which we are not accustomed to give thanks. As you compose your public prayer, are there elements in the lives of your church members that call for gratitude? Is there some expression of God's caring that suddenly dawns on you as being worthy of being included in your prayer? Some persons who work at it have developed the capacity to recognize the working of God in everyday but often unnoticed places. Here is a portion of a personal prayer that embodies such sensitivity.

O GOD, I was walking by a pile of rubble where they had torn down a building and it was ugly and strewn with old pieces of concrete. Yet in the middle of the rubbish where I didn't expect it there was a small flower growing. It reminded me of your presence, God, in the midst of the shambles of life, where all the dirt and debris are, and the bright color was like a beacon that pulled my eyes irresistibly. I was compelled to look, O God, and that flower was a lot like the burning bush that Moses saw. Thank you, God, for reminding me that you are always about, even when things aren't very pleasant and my world is a wreck.

A Sunday school teacher reported to her pastor an experience that was similar. The Sunday morning had been hectic. The dog had escaped the house and had to be chased and caught. Irritating problems, one after another, arose before the family could leave for church. The teacher was in no mood to teach and was seriously thinking of seeing if someone could substitute. But to her amazement, when she entered the classroom one little girl ran to her with a warm smile and a bouquet of spring flowers, freshly picked by the child for her teacher. The confrontation of the woman's irritation with the child's selfless, thoughtful love brought tears to the teacher's eyes. She commented to her minister that she had already seen God that day.

When you are able to include that kind of sensitivity in your prayers, you will be making progress toward leading your people in the discovery of new dimensions of thanksgiving. You need not dwell on personal experiences in the prayer, but you can give thanks for the smile of a little girl that reminds us of the love that God holds for his people—or the touch of a friend's hand that is like the embrace of our Friend—or the sound of a bird's song amidst the noise of traffic cutting through the din with God's divine call.

O GIVER of every gift, we pause to reflect with thanks on the gifts we have received. Unnoticed, you have come into our lives to make them rich and good. You have given us our families and friends, that make living full. You have granted us education, bringing knowledge and wisdom. You have placed us in a nation that abounds with resources. All our needs you have supplied to overflowing. How our hearts are grateful and how we praise you for your goodness!

IN THIS moment of quiet remembrance, O God, thanksgiving wells up within us. As we ponder you, our memories flash from one expression of your love to another and yet another and another.

When we are depressed, you send a throbbing sunset to close the day with vivid reminder that you are God and the world is in your hands. When sadness attacks, a haunting melody of a hymn of faith wrestles with our spirits, and when we are lonely a friend comes to break into the trance of solitude. We look and the church is there when we need it most, standing as a symbol of Christ. How are we ever to express our gratitude adequately? Thanks be to you for your gifts to us all! May our lives be true in reflecting our gratefulness.

There are those who think that prayer is always asking God for something and they are impatient to be on with the "more important" things. But good prayer is more than simple petition. It is sharing the deepest of human longing and thought. When the time of asking or supplication comes, it does so because the church is a caring community. Scarcely a worship moment goes by without thoughts in the congregation for those who suffer or who are troubled. Being far more than a simple asking of God for things, true supplication is the heartbeat of the church's prayer life, for it is seeking good for others. To neglect these deeper concerns would create only an anemic prayer irrelevant to the feelings of the members of the congregation. Moreover, it is inconceivable that the Christian gospel that flings us out into the world with its great missionary challenge would allow us to pray without thinking of those who are uneducated, bereft of home, hungry, sick, or mentally ill.

Prior to the coming of Jesus, not much thought had been given to the possibility of redeeming the structures and establishments of society. Philosophers theorized, but little lasting impact was made. It took Jesus Christ and his church to implant the stirring dream that the social order could feel the impact of divine love and renewal.

So supplication, asking on behalf of the poor, the downtrodden, the prisoner, and the sick, is a part of many of the prayers of the church. Of course the element of supplication needs to match the event for which a prayer is being offered. At an anniversary it is appropriate to intercede for the honorees, asking that they be blessed with good health and long life. At a graduation it would certainly be in order to express the hope that the graduating seniors will live fruitful lives, be productive, and find satisfying jobs.

Because intercession and supplication are so much a part of prayer, the leader must watch out that sentimentality does not slip in to rob the petition of its power. Nothing weakens this aspect of prayer more than the overdramatizing that comes from maudlin description of the plight of the poor or the hurt. Expressing sentiment is one thing; letting feelings grab control is another.

But we find something else is evident with supplication for others: we must be ready to be a part of the answer to our own prayer! God may say to us, "Yes—and I want you to go immediately and get busy on my doing what you ask!"

Have you ever been in the awkward situation of hearing leaders pray for the sick during morning worship or the opening of the Sunday school hour and then have these same leaders refuse to take the elements of the Lord's Supper into the homes of the sick of the parish? Or have you heard someone pray that the gospel of Christ be carried into all the world and then see those individuals vote to cut the mission budget of the church? God, of course, can function without us, but often he chooses to involve us in answering our own prayers and our readiness to be a part of the answer may go a long way in determining how God sees our sincerity.

Here are some expressions of supplication.

O GOD, we who live in this city are sensitive to its hurt. On our ways to work and play we drive over and around its misery, in capsules of steel that shut out the cries that arise from the poor. Instead of the glorious dream, the city has become a prison, instead of liberty, slavery. Tired eyes look out through darkened windows and harmed spirits wonder if anyone really cares. The bejeweled look of the city at night hides the fatigue of the homeless. O God, help your church whose beginning was in a city to be a servant of the city. Help us to hear and see. Serve and minister to the multitudes through your servant church and heal their hurts and bring peace to their spirits, as Christ did, Amen.

HOW precious, our Father, are the young lives of those who graduate this week and who shall go into new careers and work. How much we want good for them and how we hope for their future! They carry with them the vigor and enthusiasm that generates action for the building of a new world and their developing talents and abilities offer promise for tomorrow.

Keep before them their holy task of building a better society. Lead them into the way that will help them grow and develop. Give them clarity of thought as they assume the duties and responsibilities of adulthood. Reward them with a sense of achievement and a feeling of purpose.

Help us to be good teachers of youth, setting before them examples of maturity, self-control, and righteousness so that on our passing they will be ready for the demands that our world will place upon them. Amen.

Asking God to help the people be a part of the answer moves you to the last element of prayer, surrender. Your expression of surrender is the act of delivering the loyalty and concern of the congregation back to God. When you turn the mind of the church to surrender, you open the door for the corporate gift of the church of strength, its wisdom, talent, or wealth to the One who can use these gifts in startling ways.

It would be impossible to count the number of persons who were off on one course and stopped but for a moment to respond to God's initial invitation, only to find their whole career changed into something radically different. One thought of law first, but then heard of Christ and entered the ministry of the church. Another sought the luster of drama but envisioned Christ and became a speech pathologist, teaching small children to overcome speech defects.

To take seriously the act of surrender is to face members of the congregation with the challenge that can change their lives. It may seem a simple statement of dedication; it is profound in its implications:

We offer ourselves to your service and to your glory.

Take us, use us, and make us what you want us to be.

Live in us, O God, and enable us truly to be your servants. We offer you everything, for everything is yours. We offer you our best, poor as it is, to be transformed by your power.


Practice ways of expressing commitment or surrender. As with other parts of prayer, the more your own terms and thoughts are used, the more the congregation is led into understanding what surrender means.

Prayers often close with the words, "In Jesus' name," or "In the spirit of Jesus," or "For the sake of Christ." The long usage and tradition of phrases such as these being a concluding part of prayer are more than ritual.

Jesus started the early church and the disciples to thinking about the relationship of their Lord to prayer when he said, "Whatever you ask in my name I will do it, that the Father may be glorified in the Son; if you ask anything in my name, I will do it." (John 14:13-14)

Jesus is speaking a word about authority such as that delegated by a higher power. An ambassador has such authority. An ambassador goes to a foreign country "in the name of" his own nation. His ability to speak and function as a representative is granted by those who send him. His government conveys authority or power for him to act on behalf of his nation. Jesus is saying that being in the new relationship that he establishes gives a new authority to come as God's children, rather than as fearful sinners guilty of breaking God's divine law. Jesus gives new identity to life and this newness is identified with him in prayer by the use of his name.

But to all who received him, who believed in his name, he gave power to become children of God ... (John 1:12)

The use of Jesus' name at the end of a prayer is the intentional alignment of ourselves with his way, his cause, his power. It is a way of saying, "We belong to Jesus Christ." It is a fitting conclusion to any prayer.

# ADDITIONAL PRAYERS

## For Advent

O GREAT and holy God who sent your Son Jesus Christ to come into the world as your Word made flesh, we worship and praise you for the gift of our Lord. He is light shining in darkness so that we may have hope. His coming speaks of your continuing care and reminds us we are not alone. We honor your name because we know your love in this, the greatest of gifts.

Break down the barriers that men and women set in their minds to keep the light from shining in their lives. By the announcement of his arriving, herald the coming of a new day where the gloom of despair is banished and where our fears of being responsible for our deeds will be replaced with a deeper sense of noble living.

Long awaited was his coming; we, too, wait with anticipation of old for his arrival. Praise and glory and honor be to your name, O Lord God, most holy! Amen.

## A prayer for Christmas Sunday or Christmas Day

OUR GOD and Father, the God of the Christmas Season, who so loved the world that you sent your Son to save us, help us to learn the deeper meanings of Christmas. In a world where war is ever near, help us learn the ways of peace. The angelic hosts sang of "Peace on earth and good will," and yet the generations have come and gone and your creation has stubbornly refused to practice love and harmony. We have steadfastly refused the Christ-child's entrance into our personal lives or the life of our nation. May we, as the kings of old did before us, place in homage our treasures of life and may we bend our knees before him in adoration and praise. Our lives have become accustomed to skepticism and cynicism. But Christmas comes, and again we come to spiritual mangers and behold the possibility of the Christ-child with breathtaking wonder.

## A prayer for Thanksgiving Day

Thankfully your people come, with joyous song and shouts of happiness, O God of the harvest! How good your creation is, and how we have reaped in abundance all good gifts from the Father who gives his children all they need. The fertile earth is plowed and the seed planted, and the rains and warm days and the mystery of growth bring forth the yield more than we dream possible. We marvel at the produce which the earth yields in season. As we ponder the goodness we enjoy, may we also ponder the moral demands made upon us and the responsibilities we have as servants of our God. As a nation we need the refreshment of a clear vision of a just society where there is equality for all, a country where uprightness dispels evil, and where the people practice virtue and honor.

We come, then, not only to give thanks for the things which we enjoy, but also for the challenge which sounds before us like a trumphet call.

We sense also, Father, that our plenty imposes another possibility for happiness, and that is in the sharing of what we have with others. We would understand the joy of giving, giving with the hope that we are setting persons free from starvation, despair, and pain. As you have given to us, may we give to others which will be your gift, too. In Jesus' name, Amen.

## A prayer for New Year's Day

**O** TIMELESS One whose life is beyond measure, ring in the new year of _____ with the joy that comes with new possibilities! Unmarred by mistake, this new year is fresh and clean, filled with the potential for good. It is given to us as a gift, a measure of time to be used wisely as an investment and we would not misuse it foolishly. The coming of a new year reminds us of the value of time, and how it can slip through our fingers like grains of sand and we watch its passing and are powerless to stop it.

Yet this new year enables us to make a mark in time, to assess our weaknesses and strengths, to seek to make better persons of ourselves, and to set goals for our achievement that will make us more nearly your own.

Help us to make our families into circles of greater love and acceptance where growth and development can better occur. May we work to make our church a truer image of the Body of Christ, where the gospel is preached with its clear call to discipleship and where all sense their call to labor. Enable us to be better citizens this year, that our city, state, and nation will find us accepting seriously the duties such citizenship requires of us. And as residents of this world, may we seek to find new ways to insure peace and brotherhood among all people, that all may one day kneel before him whose kingdom transcends all time, even Jesus Christ, Amen.

## A prayer for Easter

ETERNAL God, who death cannot vanquish and over whom the grave has no power, we, like disciples of old, come to this day incredulous and startled by the claim, "He is risen!" We have seen the awesome power of death and are chilled by its finality. In all our dealings, we have seen death be the conquerer over and over until we have been convinced the last word has been spoken, and that by death.

And then the shouting of what we took to be foolish followers of Jesus confronted us for the first time that perhaps death does not have the final word after all. Our first inclination was to laugh and to ridicule, but the magnitude of what they were saying struck us, and we wanted to believe, too. Then we experienced the living Christ in the lives of his people who lived as though he were alive. They sang of him as present and acted as though he held moral sway over their actions. Suddenly what seemed too good to be true was indeed true for us, and we believed. Hope replaced surrender to death. The finality itself was ended and the last word was spoken —by God himself. And the tomb is empty and the grave is conquered, and we are victors! We join early disciples: hallelujah, praise be to God!

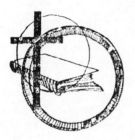

## A prayer for Pentecost

BLESSED God, who sent your Holy Spirit on the disciples and transformed their lives from weakness into power and from apathy into decisive action, our celebration recalls for us that you are ever seeking a people who will be faithful and who will fearlessly proclaim the good news of Jesus Christ. Hungry of spirit are those whom you would feed on the Bread of Life. A world with dulled senses and numbed spirit is searching. Wandering city streets and country byways, persons suddenly hear news that makes life thrilling! In this time, send again your Holy Spirit to refresh and restore your church. With clear voice and united witness, enpower your church to speak again the penetrating word of the Savior!

Take away our timidity. Sweep away our assumptions that all have heard the gospel because we have heard it so often. Where we are divided, weld us together into one church, with unified concern for the lost world. Beautify our diversity so it speaks of the freedom of those who follow Christ. Send forth your Holy Spirit again, O God. Send forth your Spirit again! Amen.

# A prayer for Independence Sunday

O GOD of the free, we worship you for your gift of this great land! "In God we trust" indeed should be inscribed for all to see, for your hand has guided us and we praise you as the Father of this nation. What great gifts you have placed before this country, and what great leaders you have raised up. We think on those heroic spirits that dared the wild seas to seek a new land and those who gave up home and kin to seek freedom.

Our land teems with good. Cattle graze on a thousand hills. Our fields grow yellow with the harvest and our trees bend with luscious fruit. Our flocks abound, and our earth is filled with the resources we have needed.

Yet in a land that seeks justice for all the search for justice must go on that all may possess it. Vigilant citizens always must watch to see that the tyrant does not sweep into power. Keep us ever mindful of the awesome responsibility of our citizenship. Save us, lest we come to despise that which was purchased at a great price.

In a land of abundance there are those who yet hunger and are in need. See and aid the efforts of those who care that the poor are helped, the hurt are healed, and the sick are made well.

In our mindfulness of the material prosperity that surrounds us, remind us constantly of our heritage, of those spiritual qualities that enabled those who have come before us to prevail over hardship and difficulty.

Forge of us a nation of which you can rightfully be proud. Make us a people of good and righteousness. Help us tend this land as a trust, given by you. In the search for freedom and justice, let us never rest until we behold freedom's dream burst as the sun from the clouds of storm. Amen.

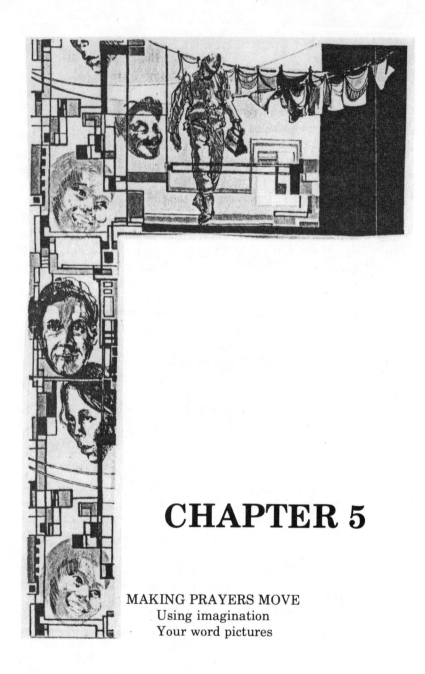

# CHAPTER 5

MAKING PRAYERS MOVE
    Using imagination
    Your word pictures

HAVE YOU ever sat in a worship service and thought the prayer would never end? You may have had such feelings and been stung by guilt because you were suffering through a prayer that was dull and boring. You wished you could do something and vowed you would try to avoid the practices that were lulling you to sleep. You felt guilty because you sensed prayer was designed to be more vital and compelling, yet in that instance it was an annoyance. A mood of resignation may have settled over the congregation at the time of prayer because the leader was a good person but inept at guiding the congregation in prayer.

When we analyze why some prayers make persons drowsy, we find that it is not simply the length of the prayer, but is also the lack of freshness and imagination. Some prayers are offered on behalf of a captive audience that has no intention of walking out, but which can fight back by putting its collective mind in neutral and coasting through prayer time. Small wonder that such prayers are not healing agents! Dull, uncreative public prayers serve only to make the congregation wary of prayer time and thus misuse a time intended for closeness and intimacy with God.

Without attempting to be dramatic, the one at the prayer table will vary the content and format if he or she is thoughtful and wise.

Imagination is both a gift and a skill. Children are blessed with imagination and use it almost without trying. They are able to see what older persons cannot because youngsters allow imagination to hold sway over the world of reality. A flower offers a spectacle to a young mind and clouds are fleecy ships to a daydreaming youth because imagination is allowed to play its role and be enjoyed.

Unfortunately, growing older carries with it the risk of a preoccupation with a mass of concerns that tends to stifle the ability to dream. The only solution for those of us who have lost this native gift is for us to cultivate the capacity to envision the world in new ways. We have to relearn what we have forgotten and the degree of success we have will determine how alive we can make our prayers.

For example, one church person from time to time frames the pastoral prayer in the setting of a short conversation with God, skillfully using words and images that make the congregation feel God is sitting in one of the pulpit chairs nearby. As a method it would not be prudent to use that format every week because overuse would rob the method of its unusual character. But on occasion it is found in the worship setting as a fine-tuned mode of prayer and the people are richer for it.

The so-called "bidding prayer" can also be used effectively from time to time as a means of varying the prayer program of a church. Using this type of prayer, the leader prepares the subjects for which is desired. The leader invites the congregation to pray silently. "Let us worship and praise God." Then silence. Then the leader could say, "Let us confess our sins and unworthiness." Another period of silence. "Let us give thanks to God for his goodness." More silence. And so on. As a departure from spoken public prayers, the bidding prayer gives the members a chance to be partners with the leader in the formation of the pastoral prayer. The leader's words focus the attention of the members on the topics; the members provide the content. The leader will want to be careful of how much time is allowed in the silent intervals. Total elapsed time should not exceed a prayer that would be offered verbally by the leader.

If your congregation has not been accustomed to the bidding prayer, members will need to become familiar with periods of silence. With occasional usage members come to accept the time when no one is speaking and often express gratitude for it.

A leader who will be leading by a spoken prayer will discover quickly the difficulties posed by the spoken word in prayer. The leader will be guiding the collective mind and thought of the people by nonvisual communication. Heads will be bowed and eyes closed so even facial expressions of the leader will not be seen. The words will have to project on the darkened screen of the mind such pictures as the leader would have the congregation experience. The use of imagination, the creation of images, will determine what the congregation "sees" as the leader begins his or her moving word-pictures. And because prayer is not an intellectual lecture, these sharp images will define what the members feel as the prayer unfolds.

Biblical writers portrayed God in prayer as a super-man and conveyed to God those qualities of manhood that they had, except that God possessed those qualities in super abundance. It was not that they were seeking to make God a man; rather they were attempting to speak in the word pictures with which they were familiar. Using the only language they knew, they had the impossible task of trying to define the undefinable God. In order to do this in part, they turned to poetic expression, not intending that the poetry be taken as prose.

So in Psalm 89 the psalmist speaks of the "mighty arm" of God, (vss. 10 and 13) and the "countenance" of God (vs 15). All who knew this psalm were aware that the psalmist was not trying to say God had arms and a face, but was instead seeking to describe relationship with the living God. Over and over, writers of scripture were forced to use familiar words that people understood to describe God and his way of working with his people. While they knew there was to be no graven image of God, they nonetheless set about the task of making God real to a people who had trouble relating to an amorphous God. Without being too precise, they attributed to God those features which would enable persons to experience God in their minds and lives. God, of course, did this same thing in Jesus Christ.

Scripture writers knew that thoughtful use of words to create images do much to awaken persons' prayer minds. Let us see how that affects you as you prepare to lead in public prayer.

In the use of imagination, one thing to remember is that you will not have a lack of material. The problem may be more choosing what you want to use out of all the possibilities available to you. And as you look about you for new descriptive terms, you may also find that you move in your prayers from the "asking syndrome" to a sharing mood that finds its fullness in thanksgiving to God the giver. In personal terms, it might work like this:

You awaken on a beautiful summer morning. Through your window you hear the sounds of a nature that is in harmony with its Creator. Your mind catches bits and pieces of what is happening. A breeze flutters the curtain. Birds take up their symphony to greet the sun. Mist of the night has settled on the grass, making diamonds on green. The sky's tints and hues are pastels that prophesy an even greater burst of light as dawn breaks like the coronation of a king! You have seen the handiwork of God! And like the psalmist who had come through a dark night of distress, you are moved to cry out,

> This is the day which the Lord has made;
> let us rejoice and be glad in it. (Ps. 118:24)

But something else has happened to you when you began to think about the details of the morning: you were allowing your imagination to picture what was happening. It could have been that the neighbor across the street was at that same moment leaving for work in a grumpy mood and was missing all that your mind was sensing. But you were able to capture a feeling that would last all day because imagination helped stamp your mind with the imprint of God's passing.

Imagination is the expression of sensitivity. An artist "sees" in the world what the non-artistic misses. But after sight, the painter or sculptor "images" what was seen on canvas or in clay. That which is created will not be a copy of the original, but the mind of the artist will make something newly expressive of the object.

In preparing public prayers, your ability to create will enable others to experience the same world, but from a far different vantage point. By your use of imagination you will be teaching them something of the universe in which they live.

Take a piece of paper and write on it a common experience of this day. Perhaps it was a shopping trip to the grocery store. What did you learn about persons from your visit? Did you notice how one little old lady tentatively made a purchase and then with great reluctance replaced the item on the shelf? Were you aware of the newlyweds shopping for the first time? Or the husband looking for items in a setting that was unfamiliar?

Can you reflect on the facial expressions of those in the store? What seemed to be happening to them and what emotions did they register? As you begin to answer, it will occur to you that Jesus used such events as the subject of stories, some of which we call parables. He used his imagination to relate God's kingdom to the common everyday things with which people were accustomed. He directed his followers' attention to the birds of the air and the lilies of the field to teach the Father's care. No one patches an old garment with a piece of unshrunk cloth, he said, because the new will shrink and tear. He was trying to help persons understand the need for new life and how the old and the new cannot be mixed.

Using this kind of imagination keeps you where people are. It will help you choose word pictures that grip the minds of your people and will help keep their attention focused on your words of prayer.

Let's become a bit poetic and try to enliven some ordinary thoughts by using words to make the mind a motion picture screen. We could say,

O God, we thank you for your being here.

It stirs more mental images to say,

Like the dawn that follows a cold and rainy night is your coming to us, O God, to bring light and warmth.

We could share with God that life has its moments when we go no place. Or we could relate to those times when life is caught at a red light that won't change.

The use of a thesaurus will enable you to find synonyms easily. You will be surprised how many different ways there are to say the same thing. Customarily there are eight or ten synonyms listed for each word in the thesaurus and you can choose the one that will keep you from having to repeat yourself. It is better to avoid the use of words that are complicated or not in the usual vocabulary of most people in the church. Leading in public prayer is not the place to parade a knowledge of big words.

One young fledgling preacher created both amusement and pain when in the sermon he referred to the "phenomenology of the God-head." It would have sent the parishioners scurrying for their dictionaries, except they lost interest at that point and their enthusiasm was impossible to recover. How much more realistic to say to his congregation, "There are a lot of ways that God comes to you and me, and we all get caught up in the excitement of his arrival."

Word pictures make ideas clearer rather than obscuring them. One seminary professor liked to use terms such as these,

We thank you that we are not alone, for we have seen your footprint on our island earth, and that footprint is Jesus.

Literature, poetry, legend, and all lend expressions which are known by people in the congregation, and which add meaning to what is said. As you read, make a mental file of picturesque expressions that you encounter. At a later time you will want them handy for use as you are trying to find just the right way to express a thought. For example, do you remember the story of greedy King Midas? He finally reached a point where everything he touched turned to gold. But most of us find that there are times when something much different happens! Look at how this could be used in forming a part of a public prayer.

O God, so much of our lives is built with frustration, when everything we touch turns to brass and tarnishes.

Your knowledge and use of the legend of King Midas enables you to turn a phrase from dull portrayal to sharp imagery. You are stepping from prose to poetry and in so doing are providing handles for the minds of your congregation to clutch. When you are complimented at the door for "such a beautiful prayer" it is more that the prayer was understood and relevant. It means that you truly are leading the congregation.

The kind of imagery that will have special meaning will be determined by the type of congregation, where it is located, the makeup of the people, and the way in which the church sees itself. Sometimes it becomes necessary to make intentional efforts to be sure that word pictures fit the experience of the members. A great deal of the Bible is written in the context of the wilderness/agricultural setting. For persons whose main time is spent in large cities, references to farming and herding may be understood, but may miss being internalized by the hearers. Inner city children may have very limited knowledge of what cattle look like in the flesh and may have no contact with farming. Their world is paved streets, gymnasiums, and highrise housing. Your word pictures may need to be fashioned around what you perceive to be their basic experiences.

The request of the disciples that led to Jesus' giving what we call "The Lord's Prayer" was really a call for Jesus to teach them to pray in a fashion comfortable to common people. His response might have been far different had the inquirers been sincere and humble scribes or Pharisees wanting to deepen their prayer life.

In seeing that a prayer flows gracefully, it is important to remember that this is caused by the leader's planning. A smooth coordinated prayer is one that is seen as a whole made up of connected parts. It is easy to compose a prayer with the elements—adoration, confession, thanksgiving, etc.,—having no relationship to what has preceded or what has followed. As we saw when we looked at ACTSS, the movement of the prayer was assumed to be from adoration to submission. Keeping that in mind suggests something else.

If prayer is conversation of the family with God, then prayer should to some degree reflect that fact in its structure. When we are sharing with a friend, there is a train of thoughts. Meanings that have gone before call for comments based on prior thoughts. We are linked together as we communicate back and forth. We "keep on the subject." We feel there is merit to the conversation if we are learning something, solving a problem, or revealing feelings. Even though there can be moments of varying intensity, loudness, laughter, or seriousness, we consider the conversation to be a whole made up of the parts.

This is true for public prayer also. The elements should lead into the next. Ideas should build and not be out of harmony with other concepts in the prayer. The leader should be alert to the use of connective words that will bridge one thought to the next, and should seek to smooth out the transition from thought to thought to avoid jerkiness. Here is a pastoral prayer that uses different ways to bind the different parts together.

TRULY, God, your name is applauded by every falling snowflake and the sighing of the winter wind. You care so for your creation that all that is needed for life is given as a gracious gift from your hand. We worship and praise you in the midst of ice and cold that remind us of your timelessness and the ceaselessness of your attention. How you watch over all! How we are blessed to know that even the changing seasons are part of your providential care and we glorify your name as the children of God that you are mindful of us.

What an example that concern is for us! Yet we must admit that we have not reflected that same kind of God-like caring to those about us. The cold reminds us of the poor who we have neglected and who must struggle for warmth. Often we have ignored those in need in our mad scramble to possess in abundance, far more than we needed. Like Scrooge, we have assumed that the responsibility for caring for others belonged to the state, and we have abandoned our efforts as helpers and advocates. The sighing wind that applauds your name also haunts our conscience and stirs our memories of those whom Christ came to serve. Forgive us for our hardness of heart, O Lord, and for our inability to see and feel, and our not knowing the spirit of Christ.

For that same Christ would have us rise and go again, and we sense the glow of opportunity and other chances that await. How he empowers us to want better things, to strive for defeat of that which keeps persons poor! And how he depends on us to be the ones who go forth with his ministry! We are amazed with his forgiveness that lifts us from our frustration and distress and hurls us out again into the world with refreshed minds and commitment. We are thankful for the renewing presence of Christ going with us.

The need for renewal waits at every turn. Our land groans with the insanity of war and rumor of war. May our world know the healing of Christ that will transform the implements of destruction into the tools of harmony, friendship, and love.

Help us to be peacemakers, O Lord. Perhaps not makers of world peace, but creators of harmony where we are, in our community, in our home. Help us to share the Christ, whose life-giving doctrines promote fellowship and concord. Through this same Christ, our Lord, Amen.


Each element of the preceding prayer was linked together with the idea that went before so that continuity was maintained. The mood of the beginning paragraph was felt throughout the prayer, and the leader felt free to recall the phrase "the sighing wind" as one way of keeping the parts of the prayer interwoven. The leader sought to have smooth connecting phrases that enabled him to move from adoration to confession naturally, as a normal manner of conversing. The prayer's balance was set with the elements of confession and thanksgiving, and the leader emphasized these two consciously because of the dismal season. Emphasis could have been placed on supplication if desired.

The leader also sought to use picture-words and words that denote action. Notice also how the exclamation form of sentence is used often to help the congregation feel God's care, power, and dependence on us. The use of different types of sentences varies the tempo and becomes another imaginative way of being conversing in prayer. Just as persons vary sentence structure as they talk, so a leader should attempt to have different kinds of sentences in public prayer.

One memorable prayer was composed almost completely of questions, with the leader asking God about some of the perplexing mysteries his people were facing that week. Unusual in form, the prayer caught the concerns of the people. The leader assumed that such riddles are best answered by him who knows all things; hence the body of the prayer raised questions with God, and then closed with a stirring affirmation of the love of God and the competency of God to run his universe.

If you turn to the Psalms you notice that many have several questions in them. Even the psalm some think Jesus was quoting from the cross, the 22nd, begins with the cry, "My God, my God, why hast thou forsaken me? Why art thou so far from helping me, from the words of my groaning?" You can see that prayer indeed arises out of the human experience as you read the words of some who struggled long ago with meaning and purpose. The ancient Book also serves to remind us that we, too, are in the long parade of those who search by prayer for answers. Imagination provides members of the congregation different parade routes Sunday by Sunday and meeting by meeting. Utilize different formats, different wording, different descriptive phrases, and different patterns, and you help members discover deeper answers to perplexing questions.

As you begin to develop your use of imagination and creativity in prayer leadership, you soon discover you are deepening your understanding of different aspects of God's nature and that of the world. The teacher tends to learn more than the student if the teacher prepares properly. At first, avoiding stereotypes and overused words seems hard work, but eventually it becomes a source of excitement. You find the dimensions of your faith growing as God reveals more and more of himself to you through the process of your searching for new ways to approach him. And knowing that you are a growing church leader, you begin to see new aspects of the world all about you for which God cares and for which you are responsible. You feel more a part of the church and understand more clearly what its mission is.

You are setting forth now on an adventure that will challenge the best you have to give. If you are faithful, you will grow in your abilities to lead public prayer and your leadership will be an opening to others to enter a ministry of prayer leadership. Here is a special prayer for those of us who lead:

O GOD, who sent your Son who taught us to pray, will you help those of us who seek to invest our time and talents in the ministry of prayer by opening our eyes to new worlds all about us? In our developing skills and perception, teach us how to see behind the masks persons wear so that the real individual becomes visible, and his or her needs may be carried before you who so completely cares. Make our minds, as leaders, fertile fields for the planting of new words, new dreams, new visions. Might we ever lift to you those things worthy of prayer! If our world is to be changed and is to become the kingdom of our Lord and his Christ, help us all to be about the business of seeking to turn prayer into deed, dream into accomplishment, and faith into reality. In the name and by the authority of Jesus Christ, Amen.

# ADDITIONAL PRAYERS

**Invocations**

O GOD, who so richly blesses us with little children, keep us in that same spirit of searching and dreaming, that we may look and behold your face, and listen and catch the sound of your passing; help us detect your presence in our worship with our children and see your glory written on their faces, in Jesus Christ, Amen.

O FATHER in heaven, whose Son walked through open fields and taught, teach us through our teachers this day as we honor those who guide the church school; enrich their lives by touching the chords of life's teachings with your presence, through Jesus Christ, Amen.

O LORD God, whose name is holy, we worship and adore you— offering to you our praise in worship, song, and prayer; take us and transform us to your glory, in the name of your Son, Amen.

O YOU who called the church into being, refresh and renew your church this hour by the purifying worship and preaching of your servants; save your church from vagueness and lost clarity of purpose and redeem it as a people set apart and called out from the world for the salvation of the world; in the name of the Master, Amen.

OUR FATHER, creator of the church and the encouragement of the apostles, we thank you for the witness of your servant, St. Andrew, who sought out his brother to introduce him to the Messiah and who found a few loaves and fish to be transformed into a banquet; grant that we, too, might not seek the place of prominence but be willing servants, working in the background where needed after the manner of Andrew, we ask in the name of Christ, Amen.

HOLY MASTER, under whose guiding light wise men came seeking the child Jesus, illumine our pathway in this time as well, that we, beholding the heavenly light, might find him whose birth caused the celebration of the first Epiphany, and finding him, may we find the hope of new life that he brings, Amen.

ALMIGHTY ONE, victor over death and the grave, in the midst of the solemnity of Maundy Thursday, remind us of the act of lowly service performed by the Master in washing disciples' feet, that we who are his people might go and do likewise in seeking to serve whoever is in need, in the spirit of Jesus, Amen.

## Pastoral prayers

ETERNAL GOD, your loving mind beheld all the good creation there is and your hands formed and fashioned the earth until it was to your liking, and then in your supreme moment of inspiration, you breathed into mankind the breath of life! You have made us a little less than yourself and given us this earth to till, and to cause it to be fruitful by our efforts and your growth. You have set us in a veritable paradise. How holy, wise and good you are! What a world you have placed us over!

Yet we are troubled, for we sense that we have not always been good stewards, trustees, of your creation. The air is often polluted and the rivers run thick with the by-products of our way of life. The forests have been ripped up and the lush prairies have been turned under by the sharp knife of the plow. The beasts of the field and the birds of the air have scurried to find food and shelter but have often found starvation and death. Forgive us for failing to remember the "earth is the Lord's and the fullness thereof." Please pardon our excesses, and lead us to good use of your creation. Teach us how to use the land wisely. And teach us, O God, how to care for all so that hunger is banished, the homeless have shelter, and the stranger knows love. Is it too much that we be our brothers' and sisters' keepers? Can we not work for a world where all find their place and know your care?

In our personal dealings, we want to make our acts and deeds redemptive. We lift the value of the here and now as tools to fulfill our vocations as Christians. May all we say and do be used to establish your kingdom. In Jesus' name, Amen.

OUR FATHER in heaven, from everlasting you are God, and you are faithful to all generations. We worship you for the King that came in triumph riding as spiritual Lord of all. You have acted through him to redeem the world and to enter the hearts of your people even as he entered the holy city. We praise you for the hope you give in him.

Thank you for the re-occurring drama as over and over he seeks entry into the holy city of our minds and wills. We are overwhelmed to discover that the triumphal entry-crucifixion event happens to us in this time. At first we welcome him; then as we understand his demands, we call for his life. But he will not leave us alone and incessantly he comes to us, asking for our obedience.

Forgive us for our hardness of heart and our false words of "hosanna" that would betray him. Stop us from being fickle with our allegience and frugal with our loyalty, but help us to love him as he loves us.

Save us from setting ourselves as his judges, and as the judges of our neighbors. Grant us warmth of spirit and generosity of mood that will welcome all to our circle of friendship and concern. Make us a people that will reach out with hands that speak of the including mind.

Grant us the ability to see others as you see them. We want to look beyond the outer appearances to see the mind and spirit. We want to be able to pierce through repulsive deeds to behold that which love in each one and we want to be able to call forth that good that resides there, that the marvel of new life will be repeated.

To this task we dedicate ourselves with the knowledge that to take this seriously will mean sacrifice on our part. We will have to learn forgiveness and will have to overlook hurts and slights. We will have to turn unkind words aside with a smile. We will need to discipline ourselves to pray for our enemies. By your power at work within us, Father, we shall be what you would have us be, in Christ, Amen.

## Offertory prayers

TIME, talent, and treasure belong to you, O God, and we return for the use of your kingdom this offering. This sacred trust we accept in the gifts that have been given us and so we offer upon your altar these offerings with grateful hearts, in the name of Jesus Christ, Amen.

OUR hearts burst with gratitude, our Father, at the salvation given us through Jesus Christ! We scarcely can understand the dimensions of your grace that forgives us without our earning forgiveness, that grants merit though our lives deny goodness, and that sets our feet on solid rock though we seem to prefer the shifting sands of the world. Our thanksgiving for your sacred deeds of salvation calls for us to give a measure in expression of our appreciation. Thanks to you through Christ, Amen.

DEDICATED to your service, O God, these gifts we set before you and your people are tangible expressions of our oneness in Christ and his mission. The sacred witness of the church as it goes into homes, factories, and schools carrying the gospel through its members has its place at the top of our concern, and we offer these symbols of our work and time for the building of that witness. In the spirit of Christ, Amen.

## Communion prayers

SACRED bread is lifted before us this day, bread made holy by our Lord's sacrifice and given new meaning by the cross. As we look inwardly this day, help us to cast out all that is unfaithful and unworthy of the gospel of Christ, Amen.

OUR MINDS flash back to the upper room, Father, where Jesus met with disciples to share his last moments. Enable us to see in this fruit of the vine the meaning of the life of Christ poured out for many; we ask in his name, Amen.

BY THE breaking of the loaf, Father, we testify to the oneness of his body, then dispersed out to many that they might know him who is the bread of life. Make this bread a renewal of life for us and send us out, too. In his name, Amen.

O GOD, how holy was his life represented by this wine! As we drink of it, may we also partake of his commitment. We would count all things as nothing compared to the surpassing quality of knowing Jesus Christ and walking in his way of life. In his name, Amen.

WE, the church, gather about this table as the family of God, to eat of bread, symbolic of the body of Christ. We come with expectant and quiet minds to receive good gifts from him. In this mood of reflection, help us to examine ourselves and renew the covenant we have made with Jesus Christ, for we pray in him, Amen.

**W**HAT debtors we are to Christ, O Lord, and how we would proclaim our love for him! During this time, as we drink of this wine, help us to envision him clearly, uncluttered by our human frailties and shortcomings. May our understanding of him be fresh and ever new, and may we walk as he would have. Help us forsake false pride and be one about this table, through your Son, Amen.

## Closing prayers

**N**OW we have been gathered—now we would go forth to service—empowered to witness and to serve. May the unity of this moment go with us to keep our testimony strong and pure. To him be glory and praise! Amen.

**W**ITH the word preached and sung and celebrated, we go forth, O God, with hearts that rejoice and spirits that are thrilled with the task before us! Give us the wisdom and understanding we need to be sound witnesses to the world of the love and favor of our Lord Jesus Christ, for we ask this in his name and for the sake of his kingdom, Amen.

**T**HANK you, Father, for the gifts of this hour that we have been together. Sin is banished and hope renewed, and we feel the sense of your presence going forth with us. Keep us faithful at your tasks and keep our fellowship with each other and with you strong, we ask in the spirit of the Master, Jesus Christ, Amen.

**M**AY Christ be in our hearts and lives, now and forever! Amen.